Rural Farmers' Market

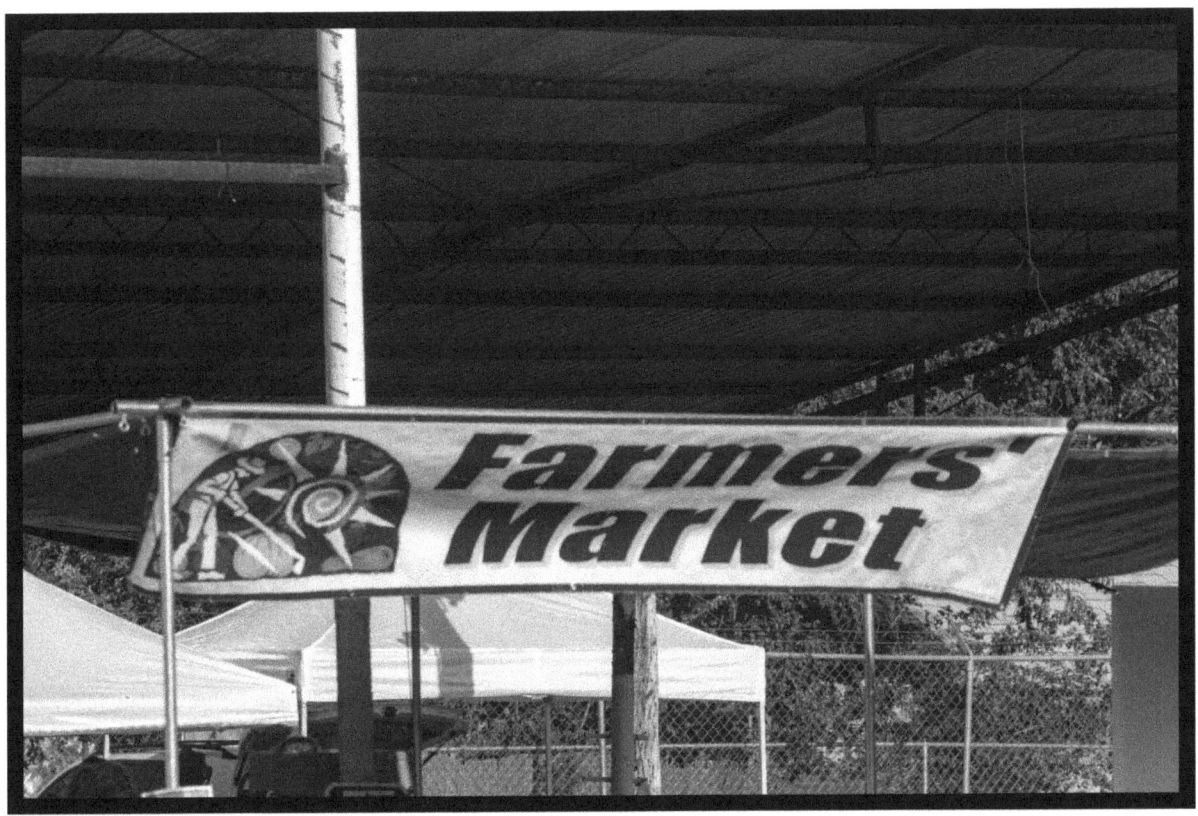

Written by: Jasper Eyrich-Bingham

Writer: Jasper Eyrich-Bingham

www.eyrichbinghamstudio.com

Silver City-New Mexico

Cover design: Jasper Eyrich-Bingham

Printed in the United States by www.lulu.com

Copyright © eyrichbinghamstudio.com

All Rights Reserved

Eyrich-Bingham Studio

Silver City, NM 88061

Table of contents

The Tool of a Consumer	5
What is Masking People at the Farmers Market?	13
What Kind of Shoes are People Wearing?	19
The Vessel of a Farmer	27
Comparing Raspberry Jam	37
Comparing Cucumbers	45
Generative Research	53
Future Reference	64

The Tool of a Consumer

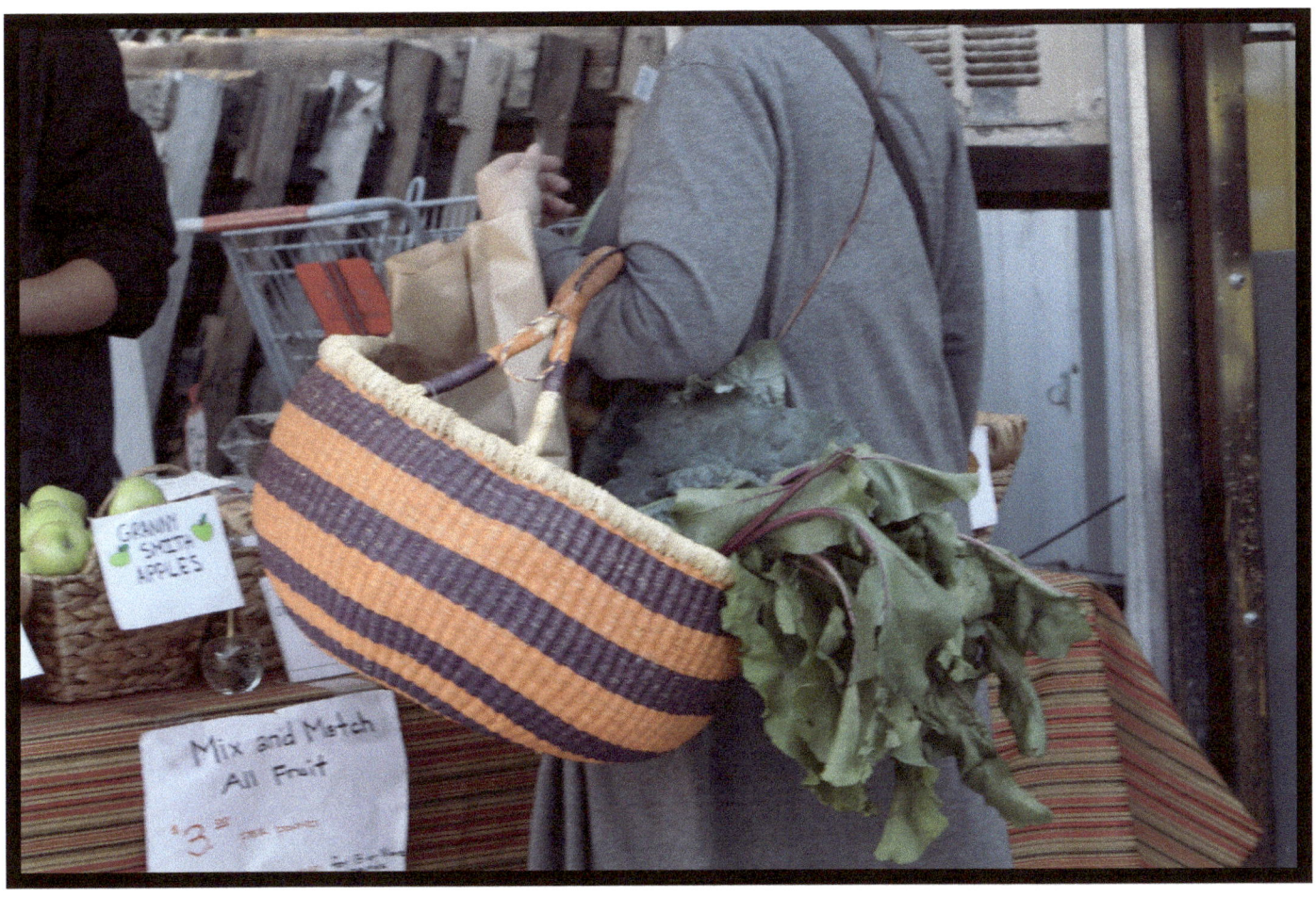

Going out for the first time to take photographs at the farmers market, I didn't know what patterns I was going to identify. After walking around the Farmers' Market, taking photos, and trying getting comfortable in my surroundings I thought, "What is a common trait among the shoppers at the farmers market?" Initially I photographed hands, they saved me from making eye contact. Eventually, I noticed what were in people's hands; the majority of people used a bag or basket to carry their goods form the Farmers' Market.

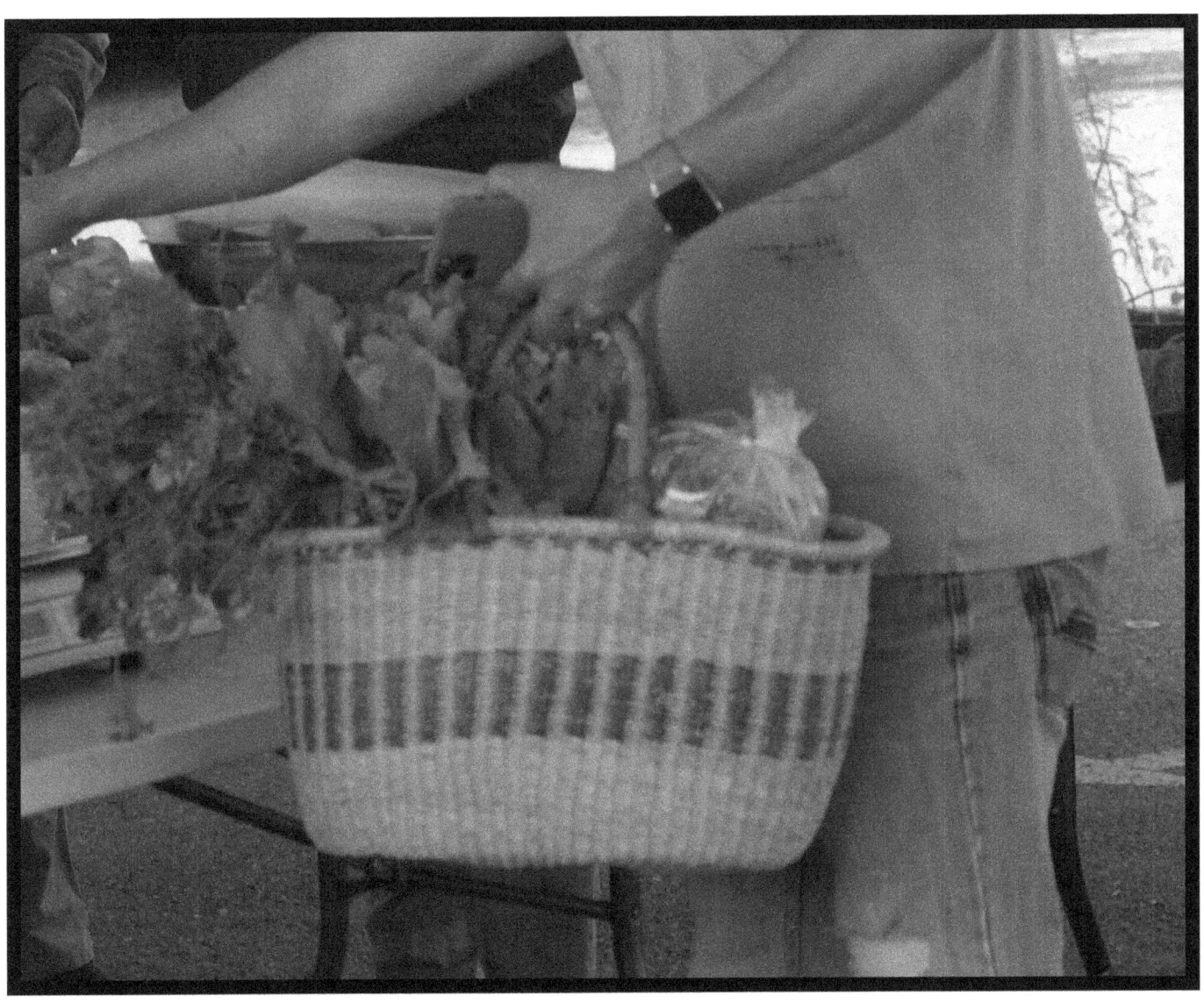

I used a Non-participant observational method to collect my images. This style of data collection allowed me to gather data without interacting with any of the shoppers or farmers. I never considered using "participation", or "minimal participation" methods because I don't like verbally interacting with strangers. I didn't need to ask anybody any questions, and I certainly didn't want others to notice me while I was taking photos.

I ran into a few problems, mostly due to my own technical incompetence – camera operation. I had trouble with the auto focus. I didn't know the focus area was chosen from the red rectangle in the viewfinder; I thought it was selected on the center circle.

Although the head of the Farmers' Market, Andrea, kindly invited me in, I still felt out of place, a stranger. I was invading people's privacy, making me uncomfortable.

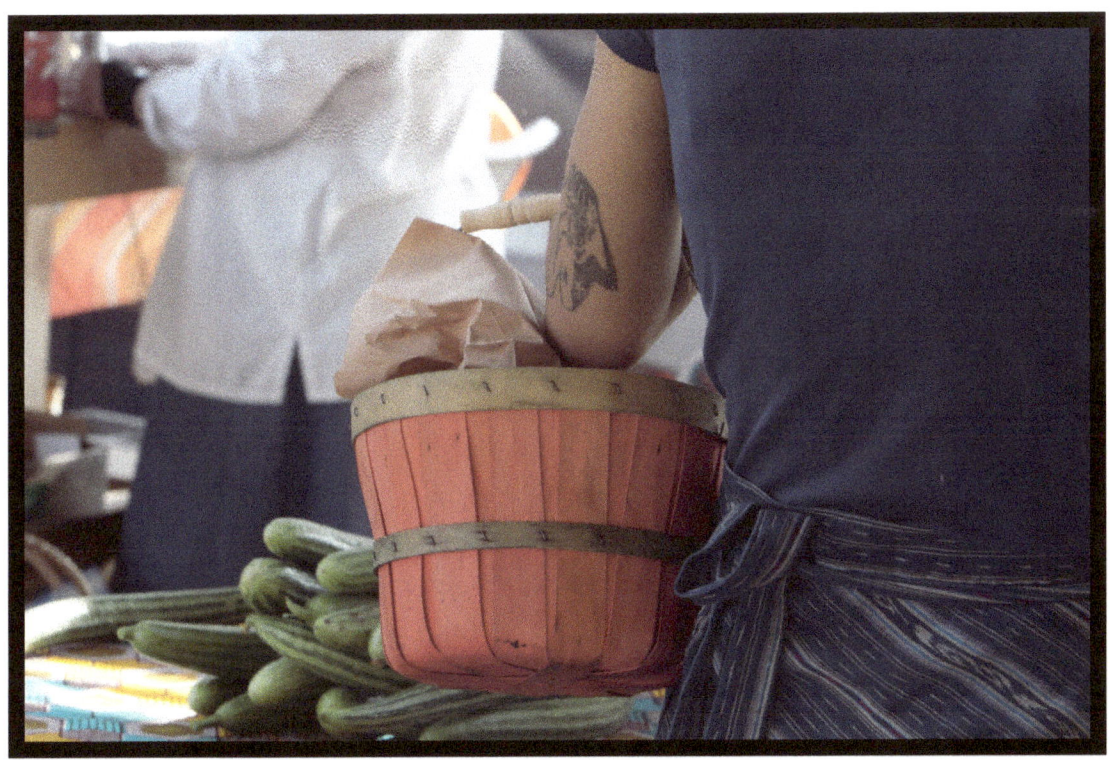

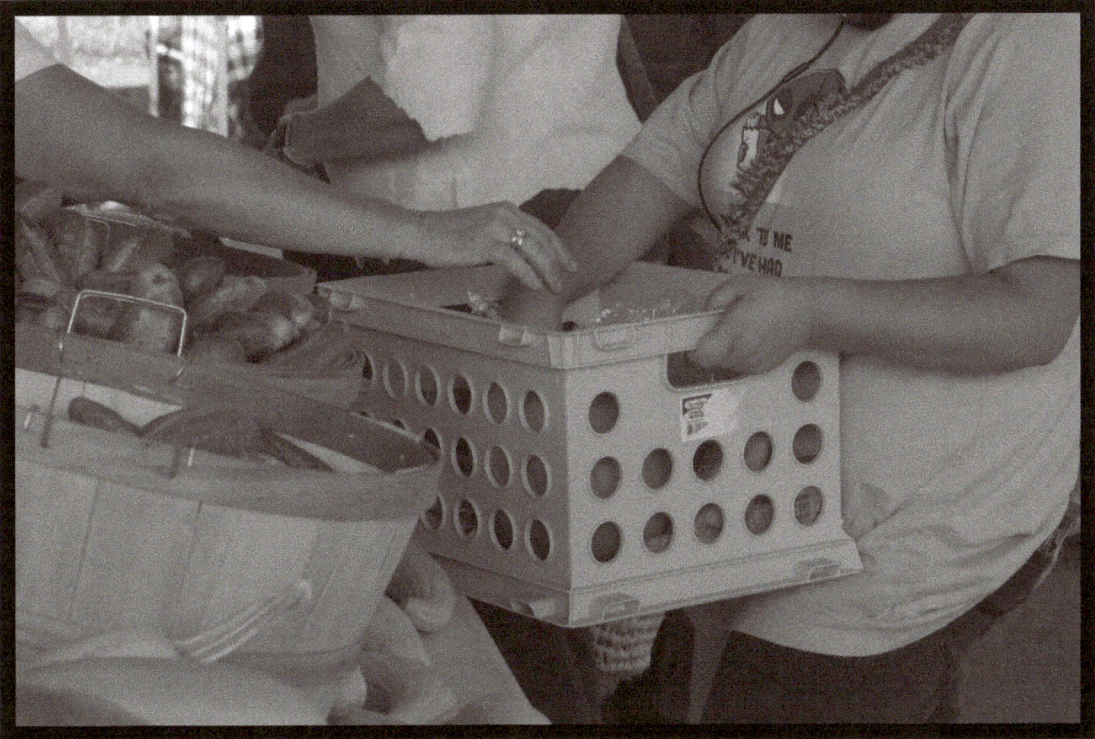

The materials of cotton and wicker had the highest frequency among the vessels' construction. There were some that were quite out of the norm such as a plastic crate and a basket made out of thin pieces of wood. I had a particular interest towards the plastic crate; it was the only container made out of plastic

My plan initially was to compare the Silver City Farmers' Market (held downtown), the Mimbres Valley Farmers' Market, and the Silver City Farmers' Market (held at ace hardware), separately. I didn't conduct my research that way. There were no relevant differences between the people, or the produce from each of the Farmers' Markets. There were universal characteristics between all 3 making a holistic comparison logical: although, I could have compared each of them separately, I thought it would be easier for my fist project to observe each of them as a single Farmers' Market.

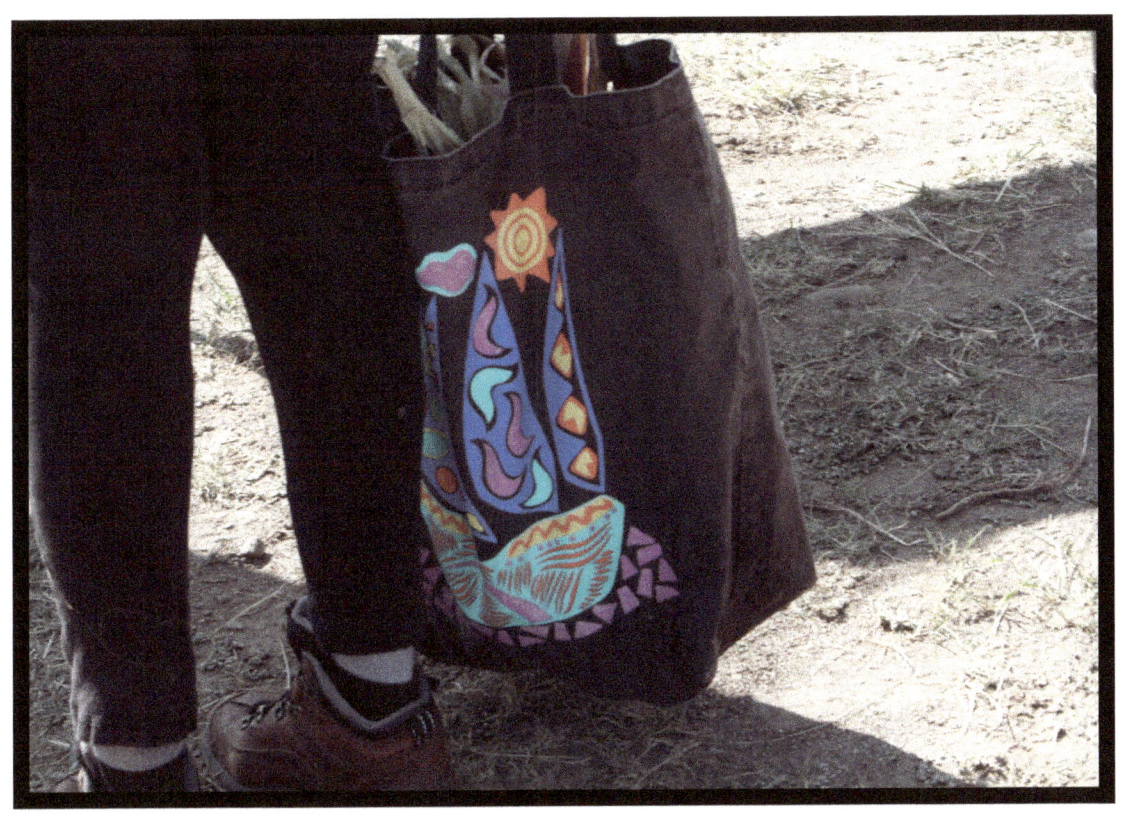

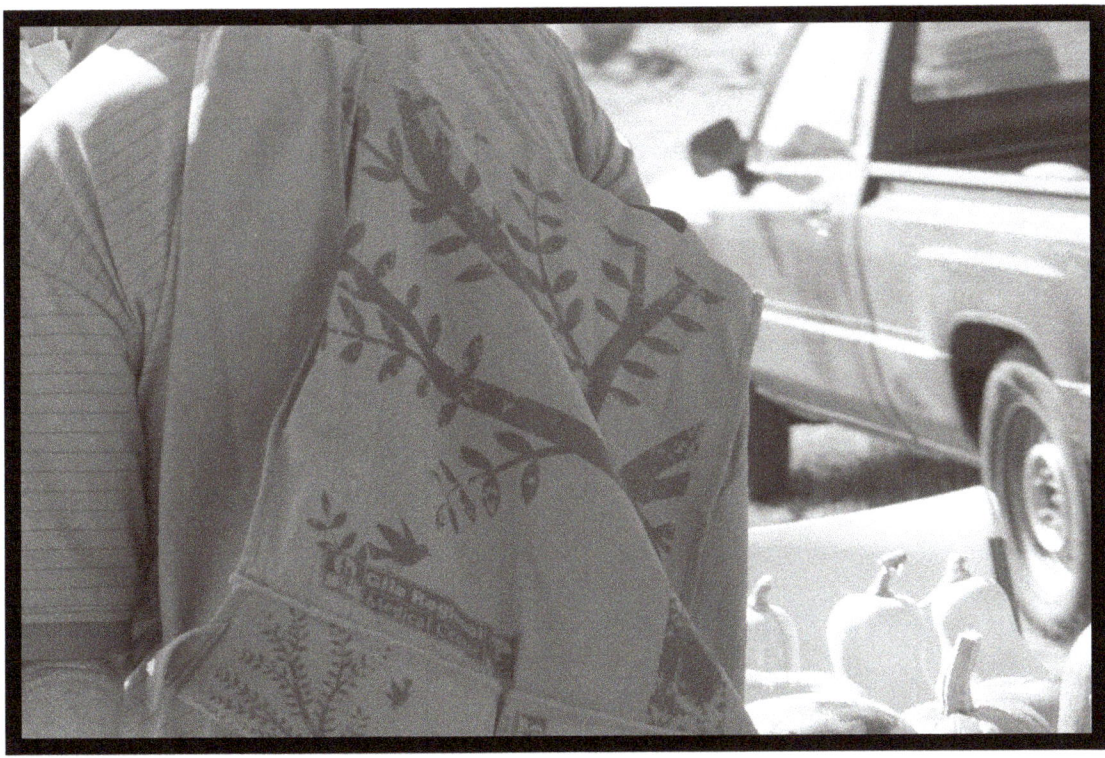

What is Masking People at the Farmers' Market?

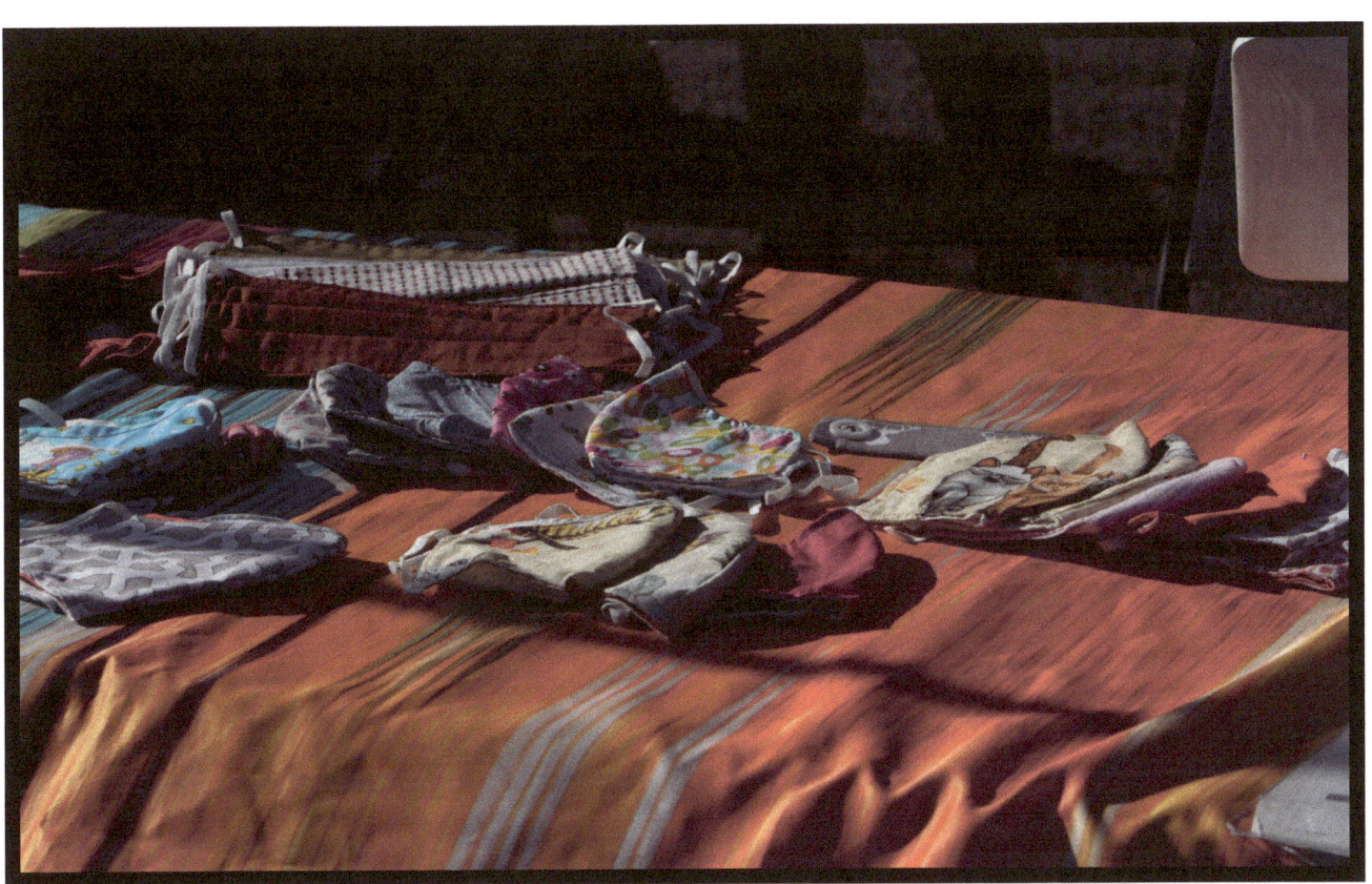

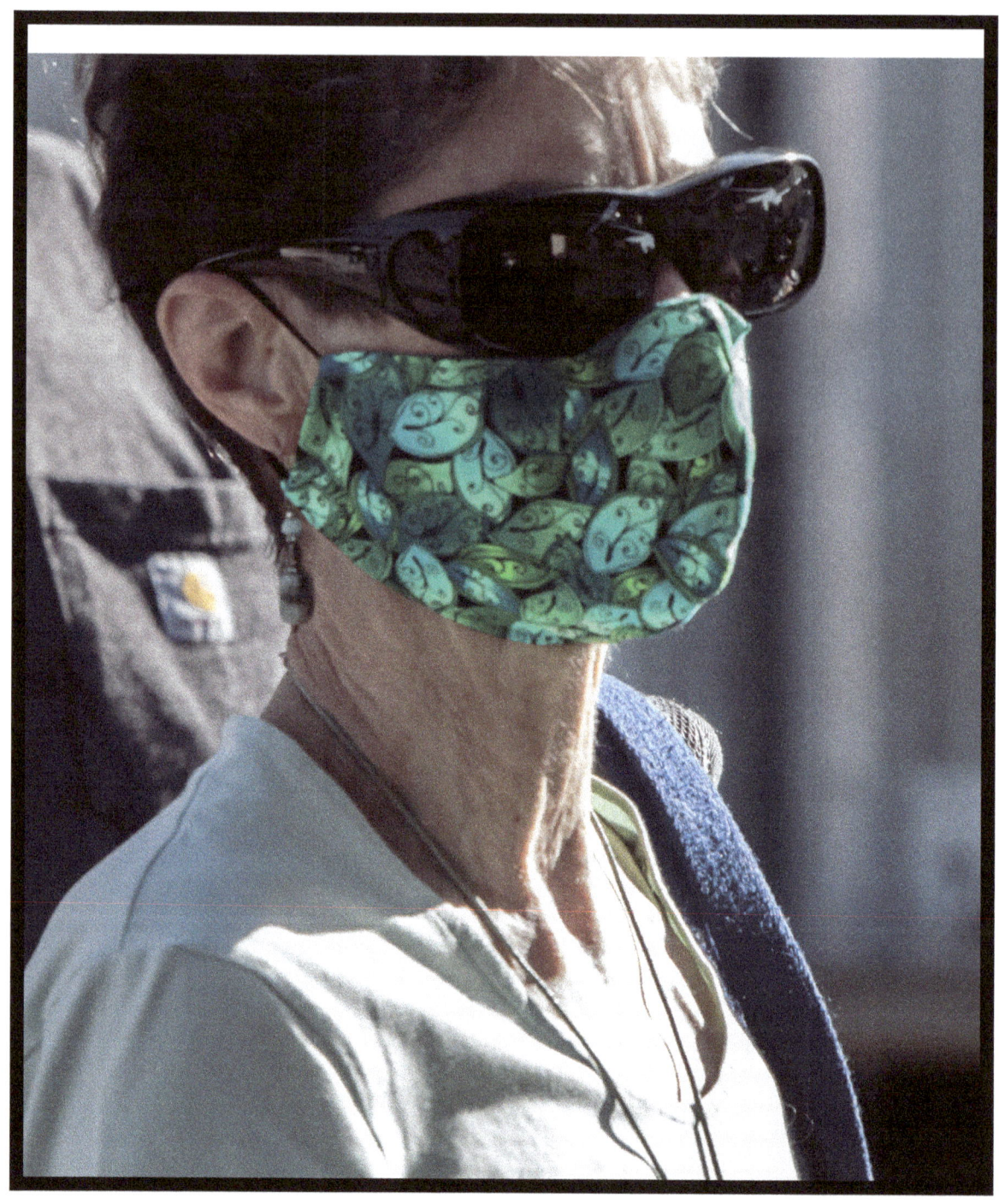

Masks were the first pattern I saw, but I didn't have the courage taking pictures of peoples' faces in order to collect data (material, color, style) on the safety precautions protecting people from Covid 19. On my second day, I noticed particularly eye-catching colors and patterns on peoples' facial coverings like rainbows and abstract leaves, peaking my interest. I decided to muster up the courage, step out of my comfort zone, and start taking pictures of people.

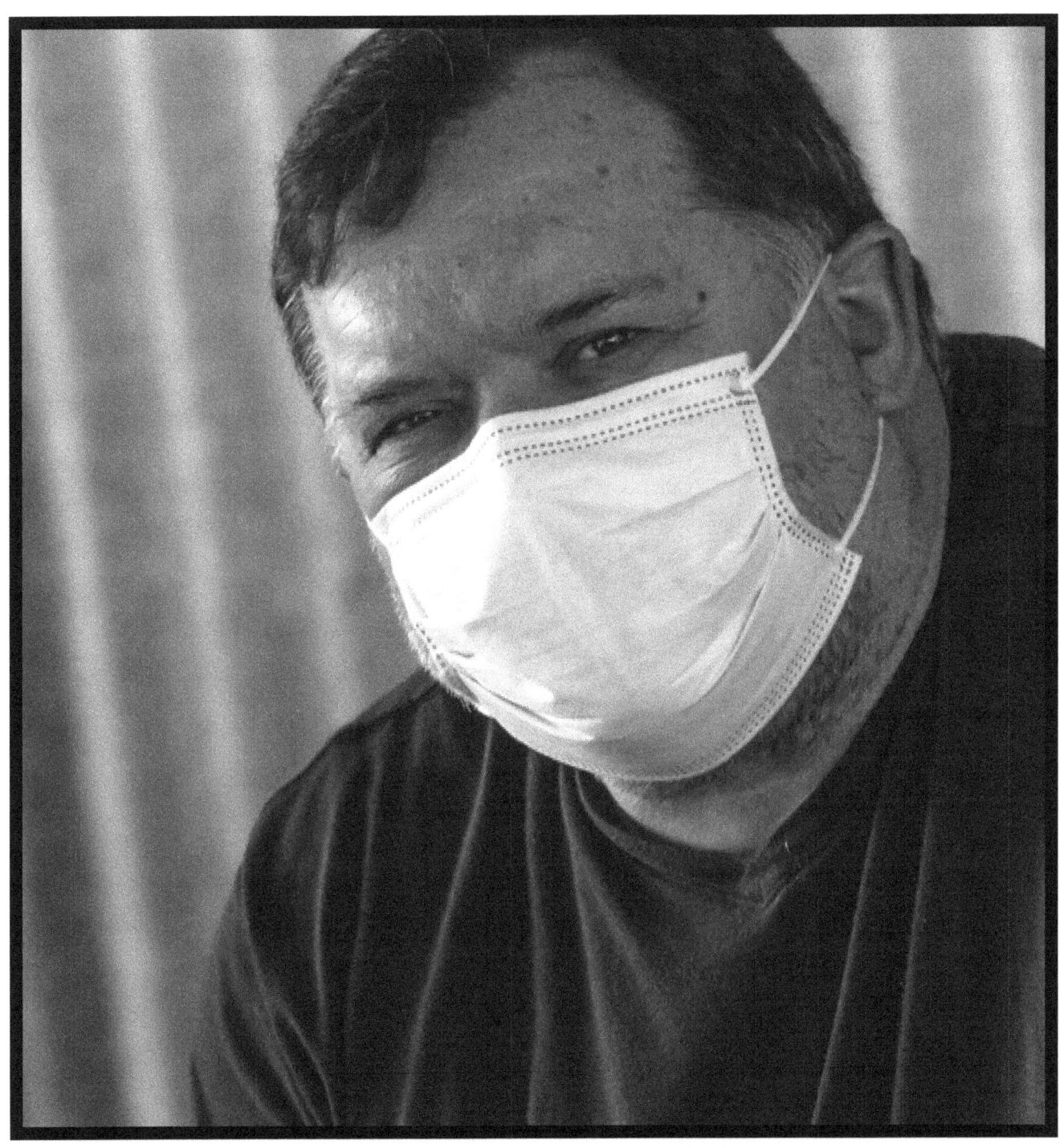

I used a non-participant observational method to collect my data. It was important to me that I not be noticed by any of the shoppers or farmers I was photographing. I already felt uncomfortable enough taking pictures of people above their shoulders. I didn't want feel more uncomfortable by awkward gazes through my viewfinder. To avoid being seen, I tried I keep my distance from my subjects. If I did get close, I attempted to take a picture of the person while they were in the middle of a conversation. However, I wasn't 100% successful. I was caught taking a photo of the man you see above, and I got roped into a conversation about his eco-friendly plastic containers.

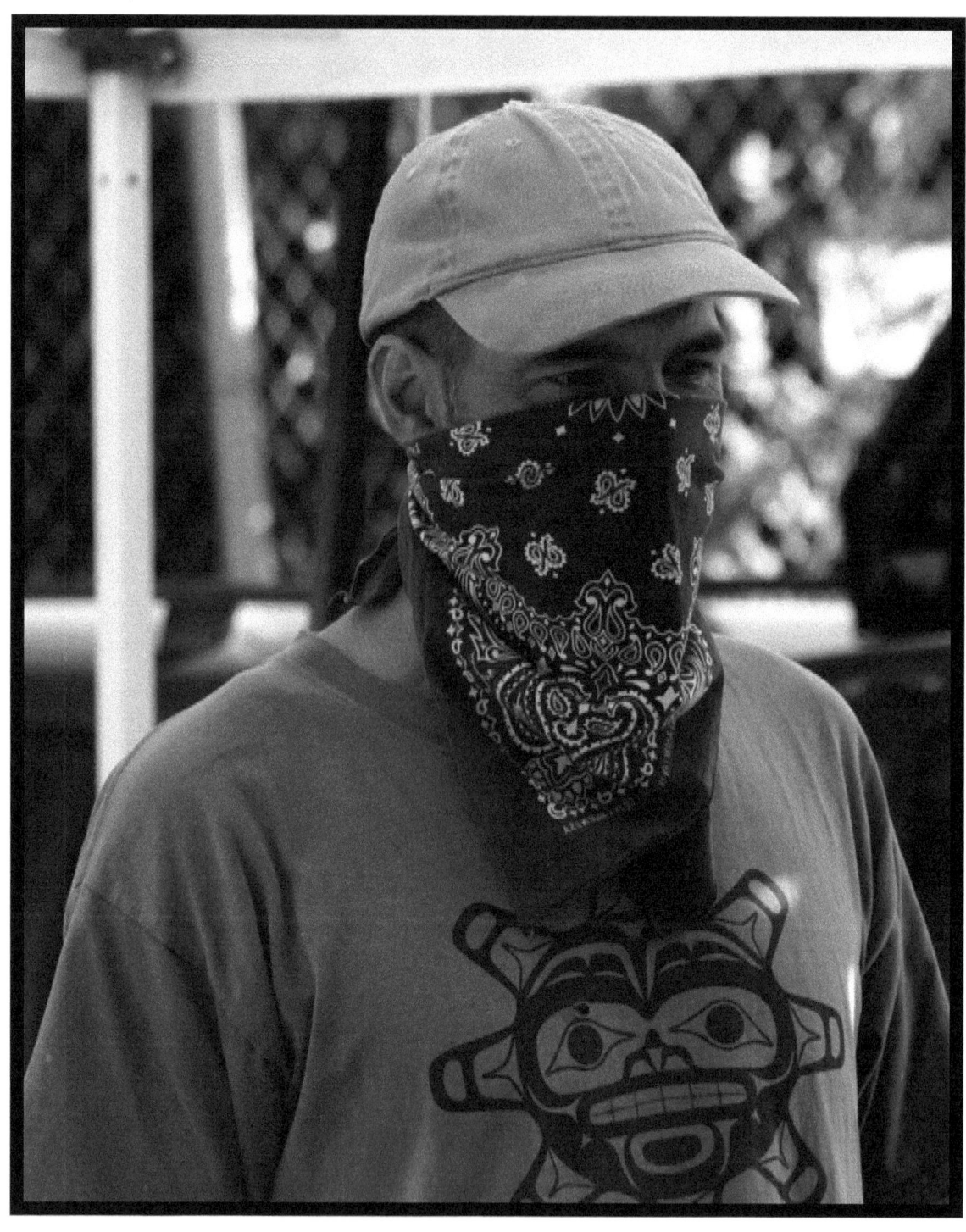

The method I used for my visual documentation provided the most challenges. Keeping my distance from the patrons of the Farmers' Market made it challenging to fill the viewfinder with the specific person and their mask. Often, my intended subject was obstructed by a group of people. I wish I felt comfortable enough to ask the person if I could take a picture of their mask, making data collecting much easier.

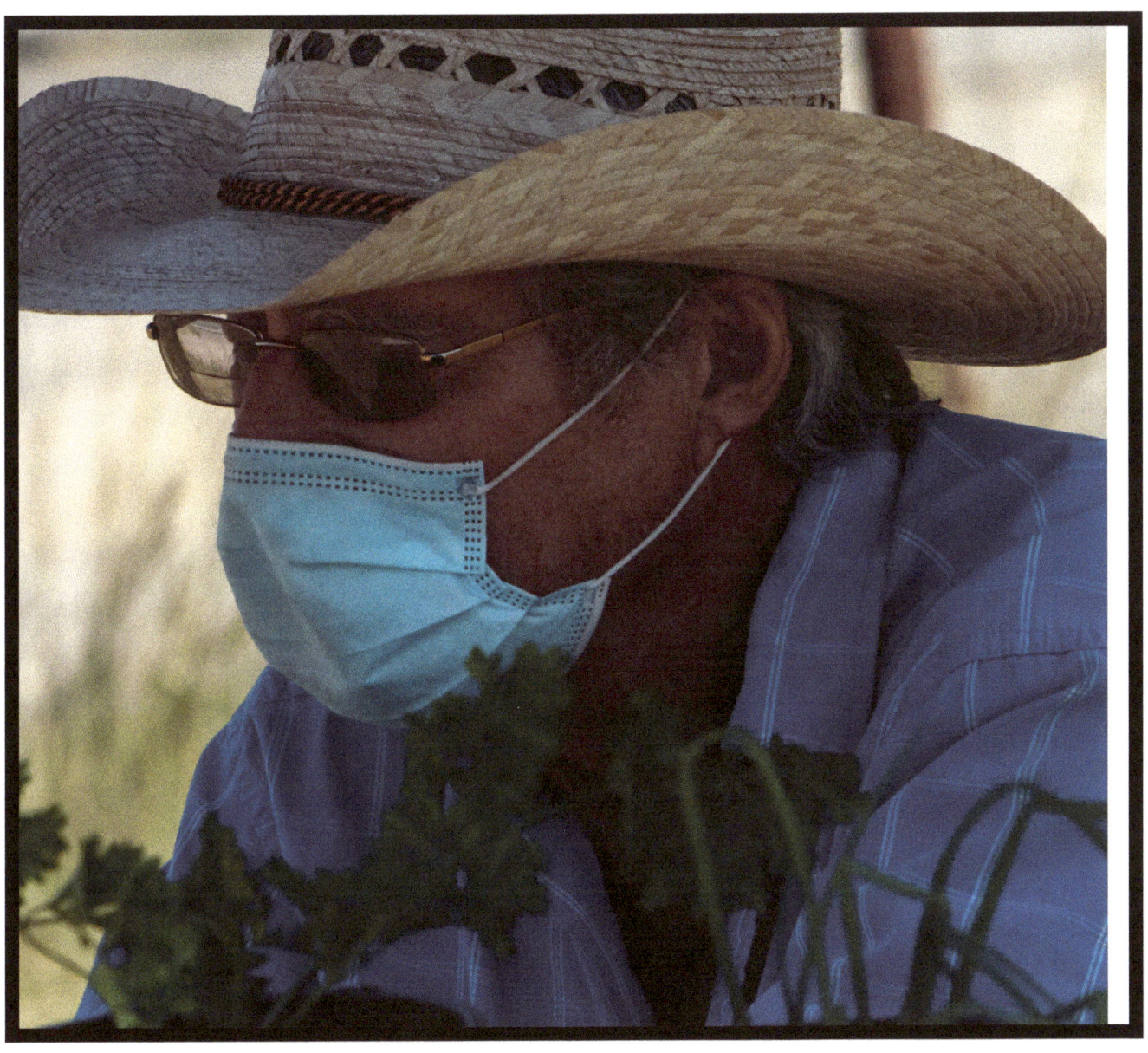

The majority of the facial coverings I studied were either made of woven cloth or non-woven surgical masks. The cloth masks were either made out of cotton or polyester and the surgical masks were made of a material called polypropylene (a type of plastic also used to package products for consumers and some plastic automotive parts). Being made out of a non-woven plastic material, the surgical masks provided better protection than the cloth masks. I was surprised by the magnitude of surgical masks versus fabric masks, because the reusability of fabric ones. Doesn't everyone want to reduce and reuse?

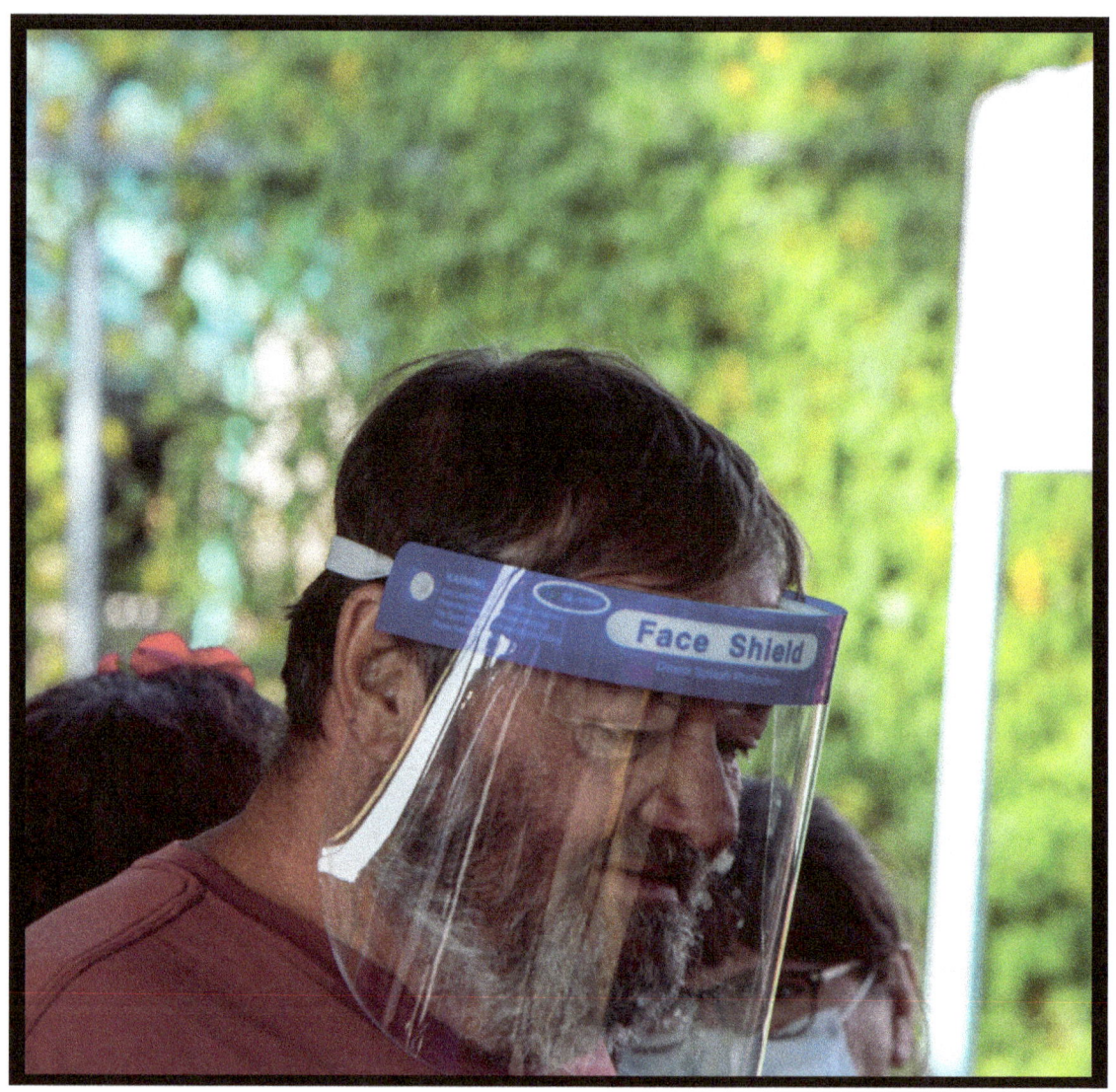

I was intrigued by plastic face shields. I only saw two people wearing these when I was at a farmers market. The other person wore a cloth mask under the face shield; I felt this was a bit over kill, but better to be safe than sorry.

What Kind of Shoes are People Wearing?

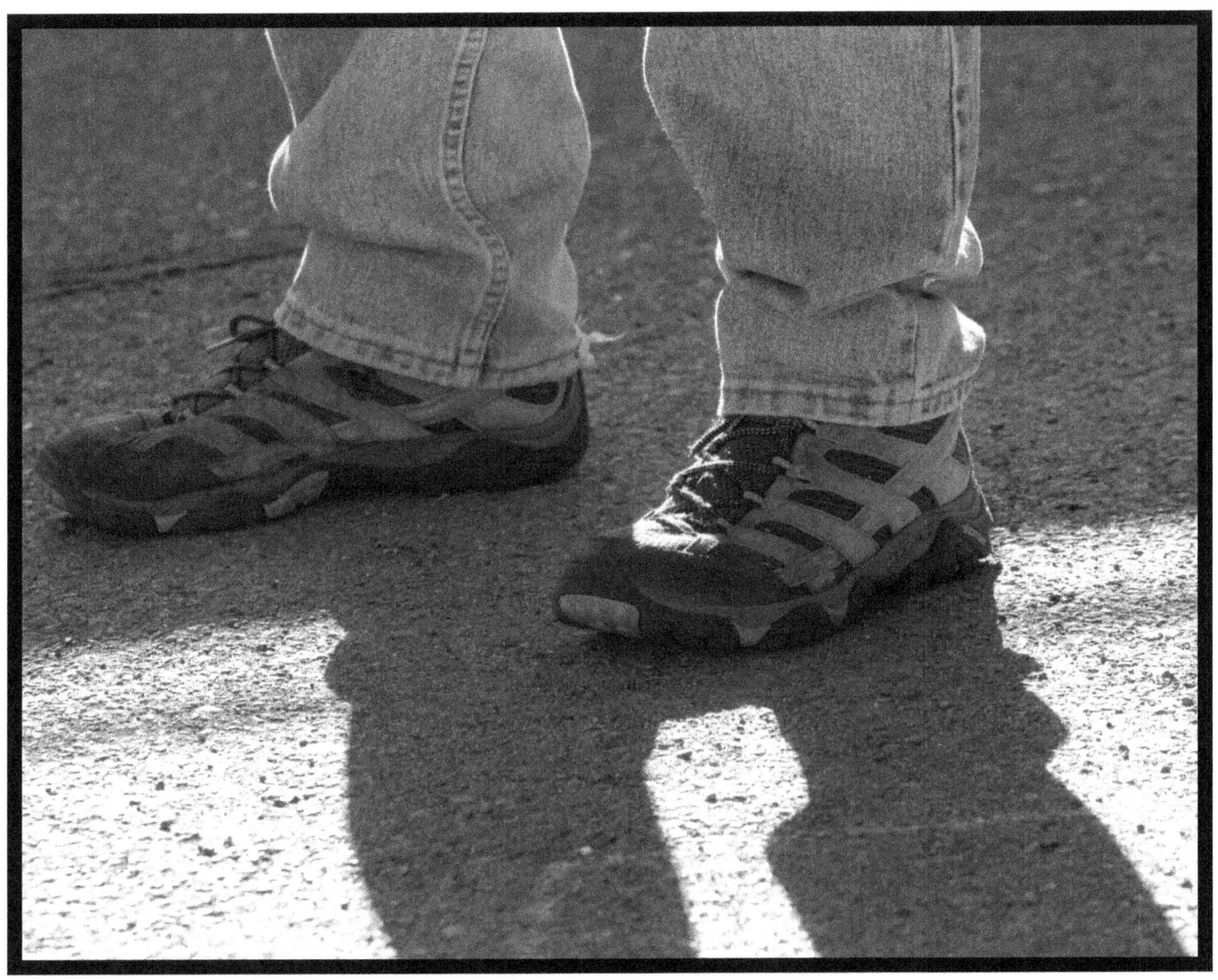

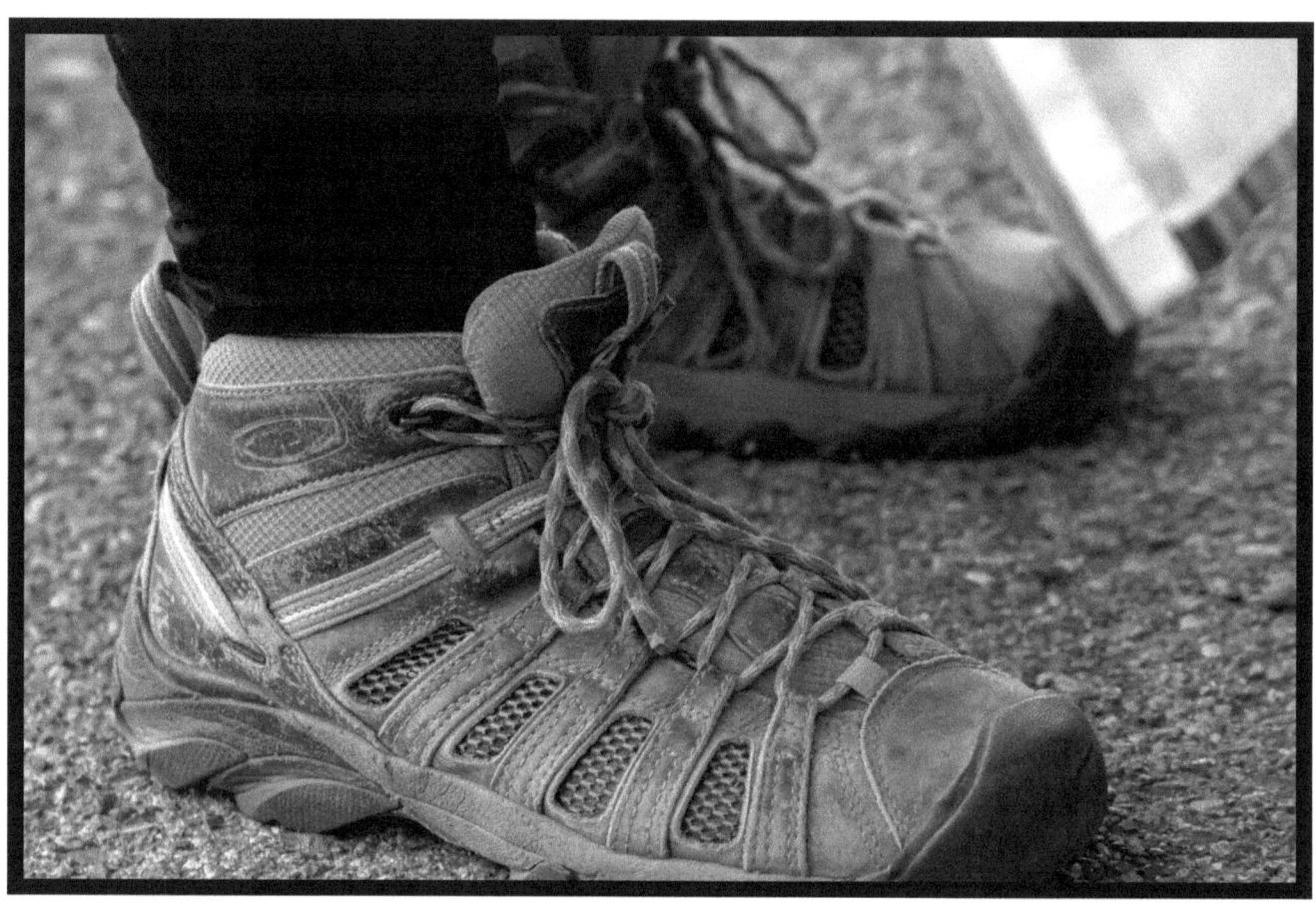

After the nerve-racking experience I had capturing images of peoples' masks, I was ready to slow down. Looking down, away from peoples' faces was the best way to go. Observing lower to the ground I saw a pattern that was impossible to miss; everybody was wearing a pair of shoes. I primarily focused on weather the individual was wearing an open or closed toed shoe. It would have been difficult to make other type of observation since I wasn't an expert on what different shoes were made of. I also didn't feel dedicated enough to meticulously determine what brand the shoes were.

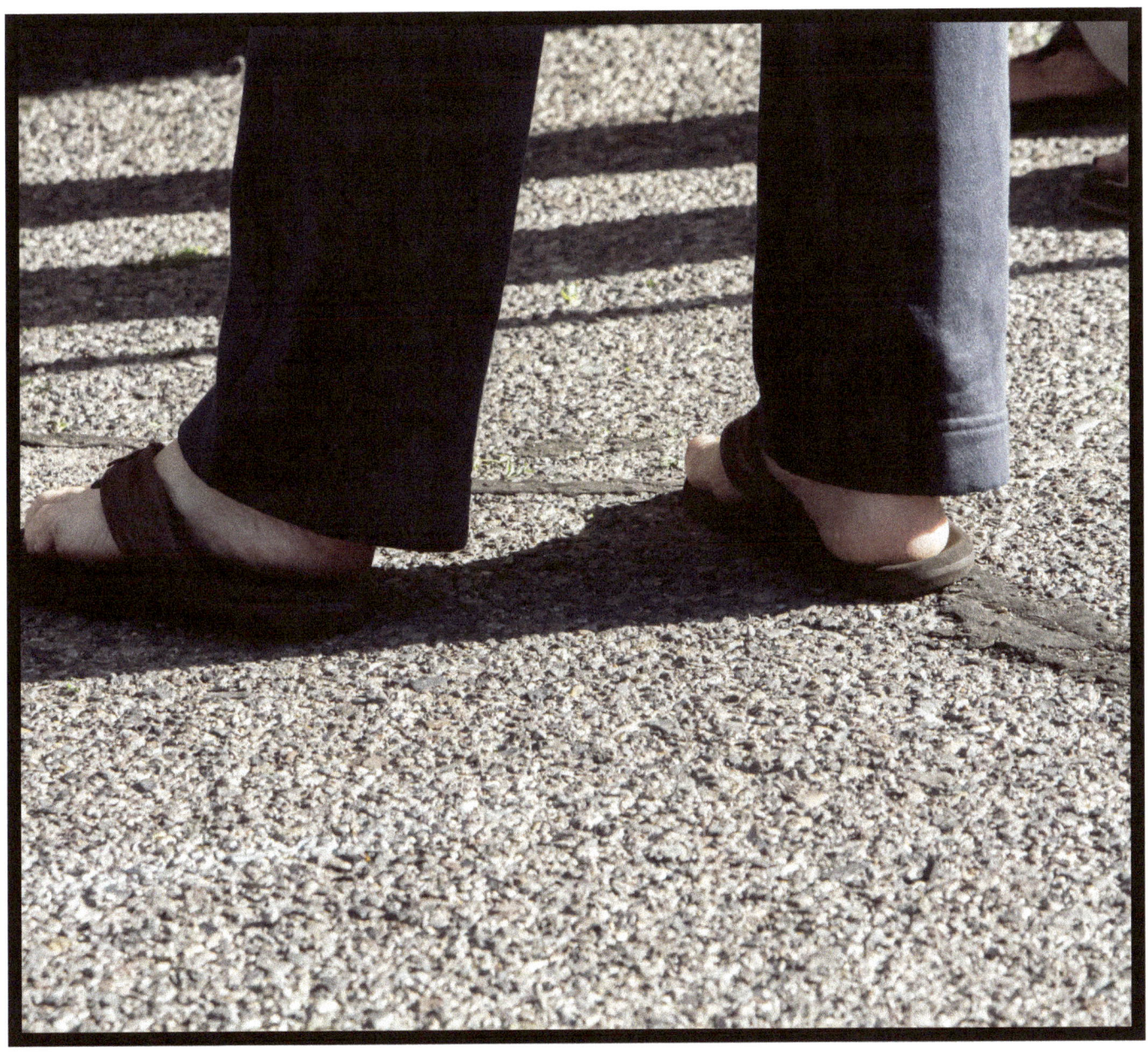

Again, I used a non- participant observational method to gather information. I didn't want to ask anybody about their shoes, nor did I think it was necessary. Although, it would've allowed me to answer more specific questions (shoe brand).

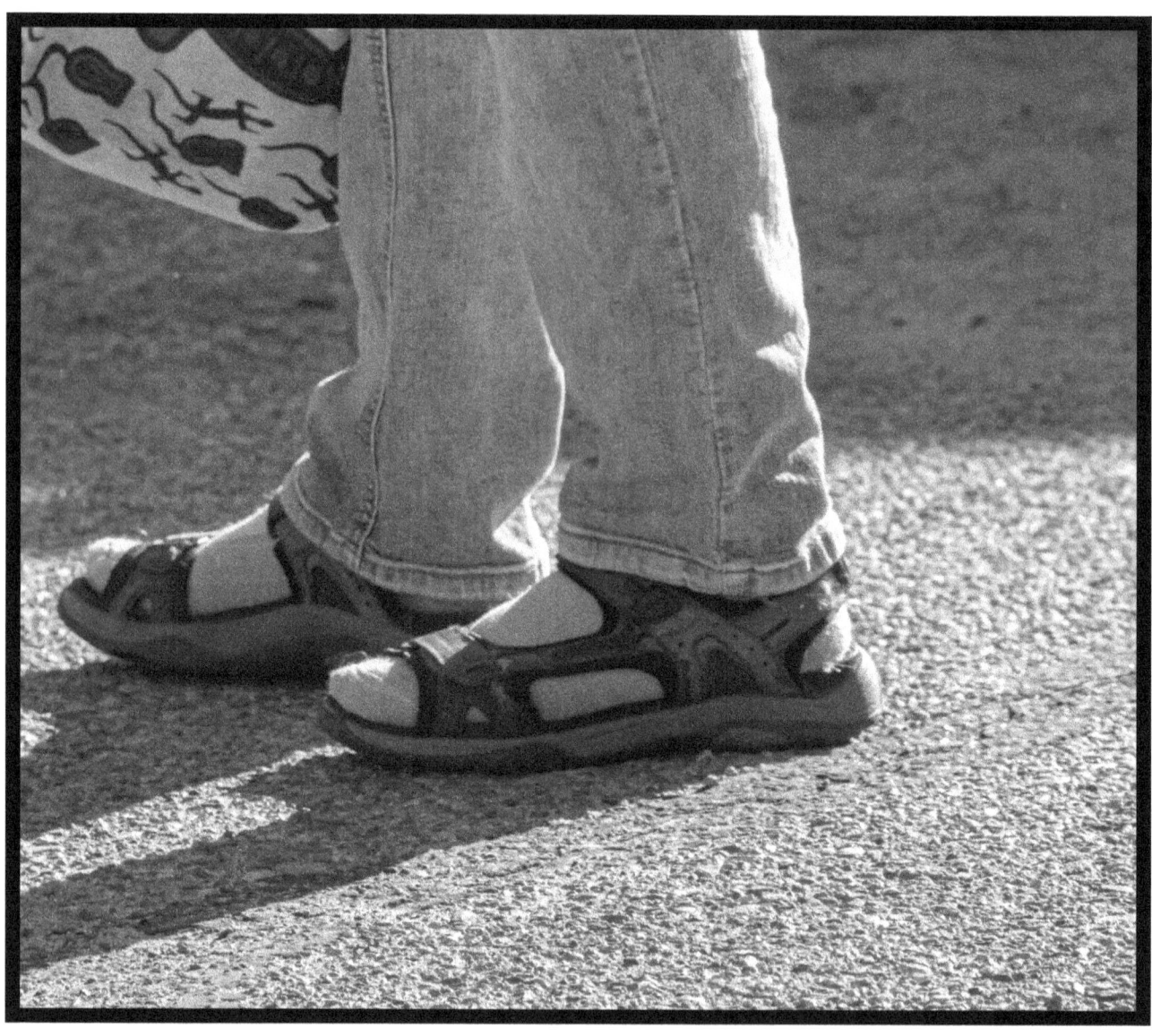

I had no trouble observing and photographing shoes. I had no technical troubles with my camera and I didn't feel uncomfortable while I was gathering data. By this point, I felt comfortable taking photographs at the Farmers' Market and accustomed to my camera, thanks in part to my photography class.

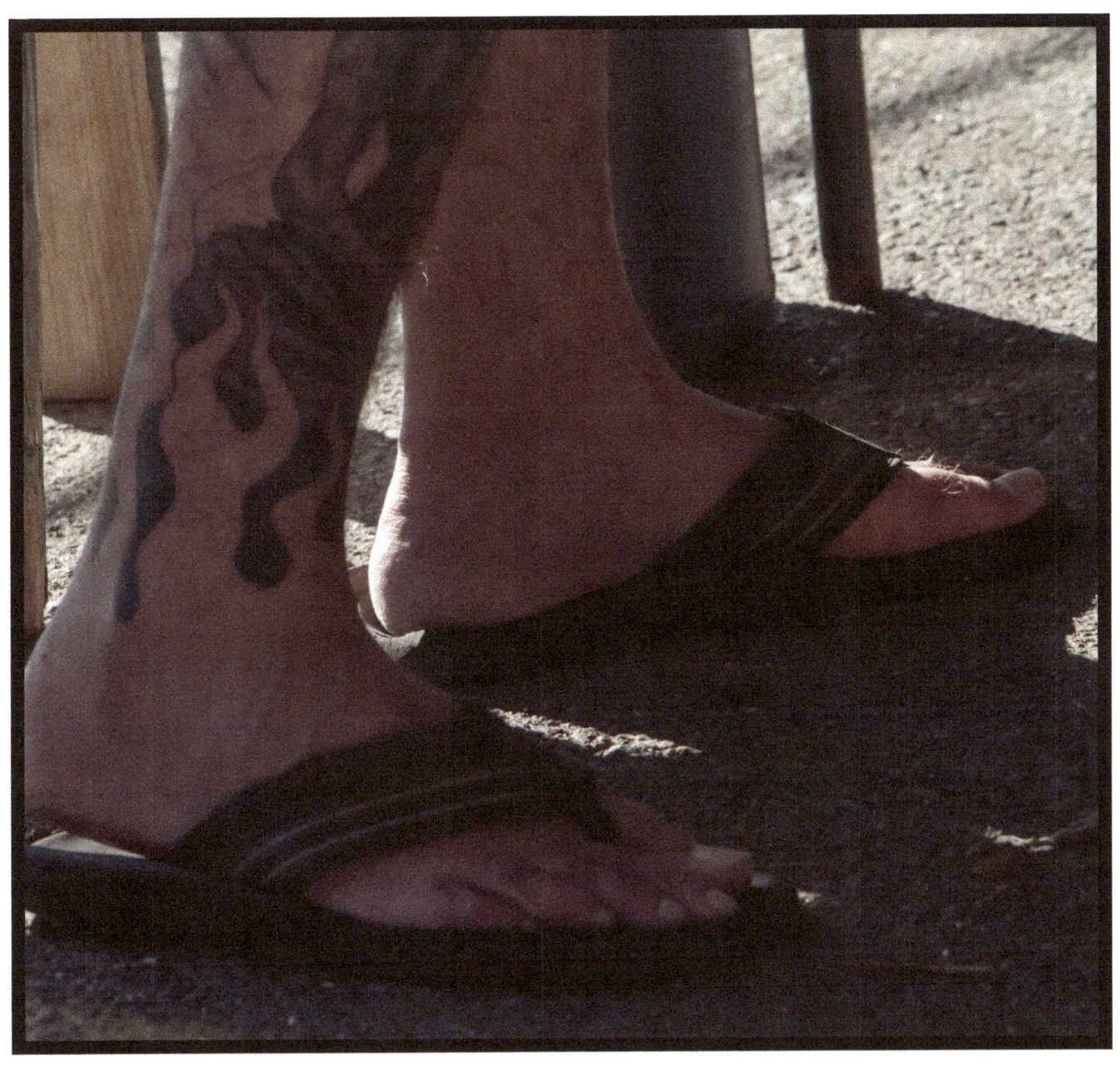

I saw primarily open toed shoes (flip-flops and sandals), likely due to the warm weather. It was reaching 75 degrees by the time the Market opened. I can't say anything specific about closed toed shoes other than they're close toed & the diversity of styles were many; I couldn't draw any concrete conclusions based on the data I gathered. Goes to show the variety of shoes people that shop and sell at The Farmers' Market.

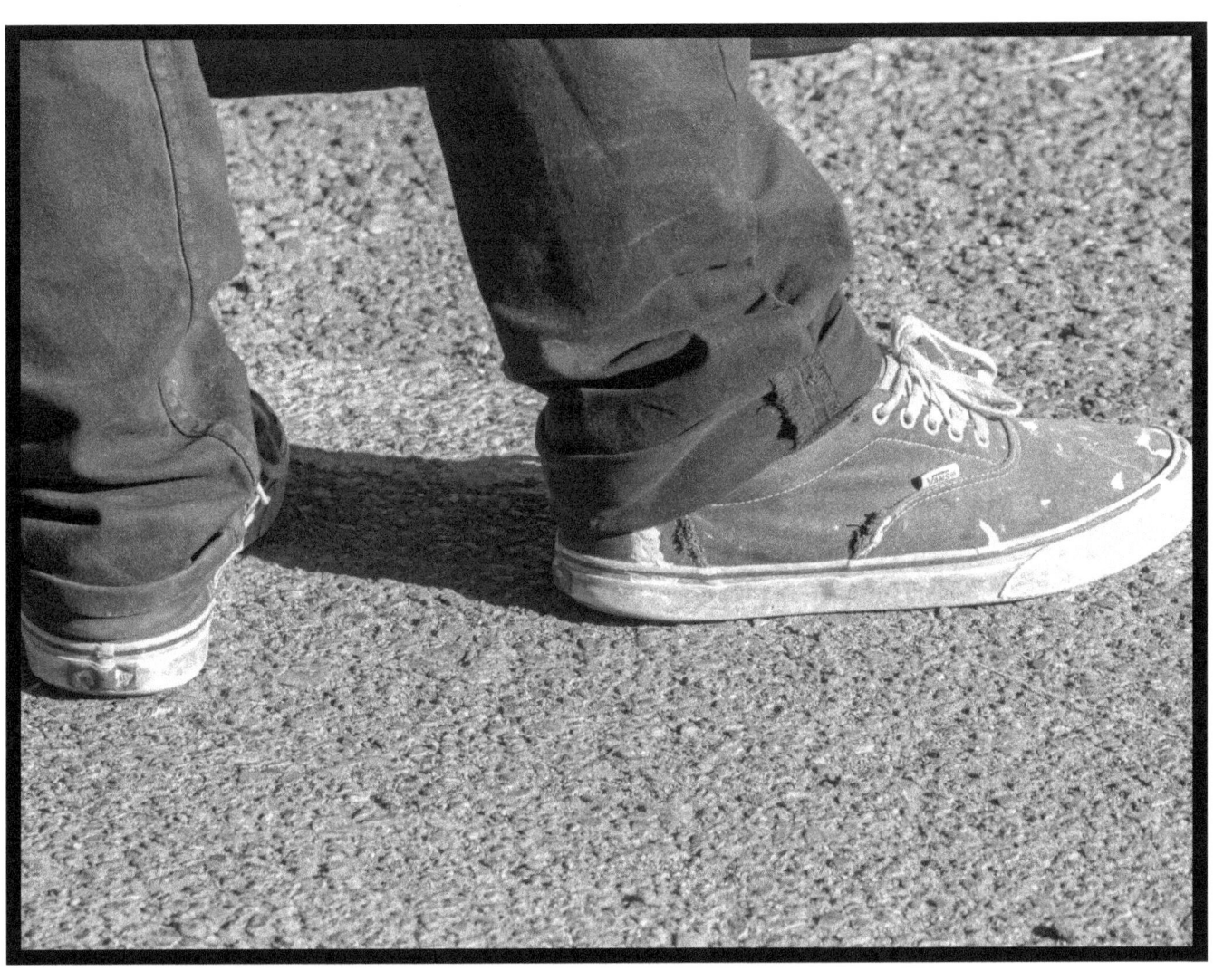

The Vessel of a Farmer

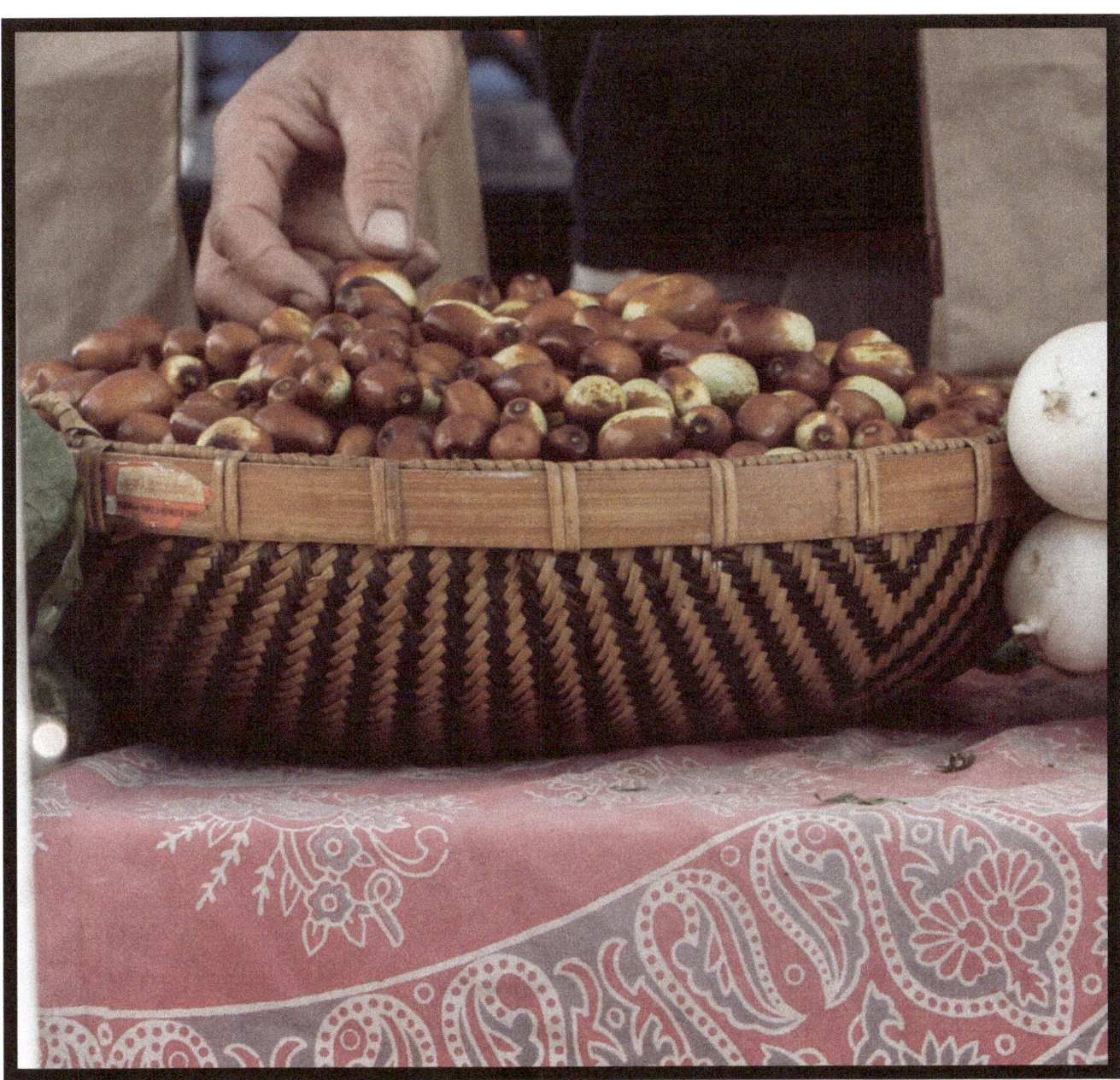

3

For the most part, I was deducing my [overall] patterns based on the buyers at the farmers market; I paid attention to them. It occurred to focus on the similarities between the farmers. It had to be something unique to the farmer; I decided on photographing the vessels that the farmers use to display their produce or whatever else they may be selling: pastries, potted plants, or occasional hygiene products. I focused on what the vessel was constructed with specifically.

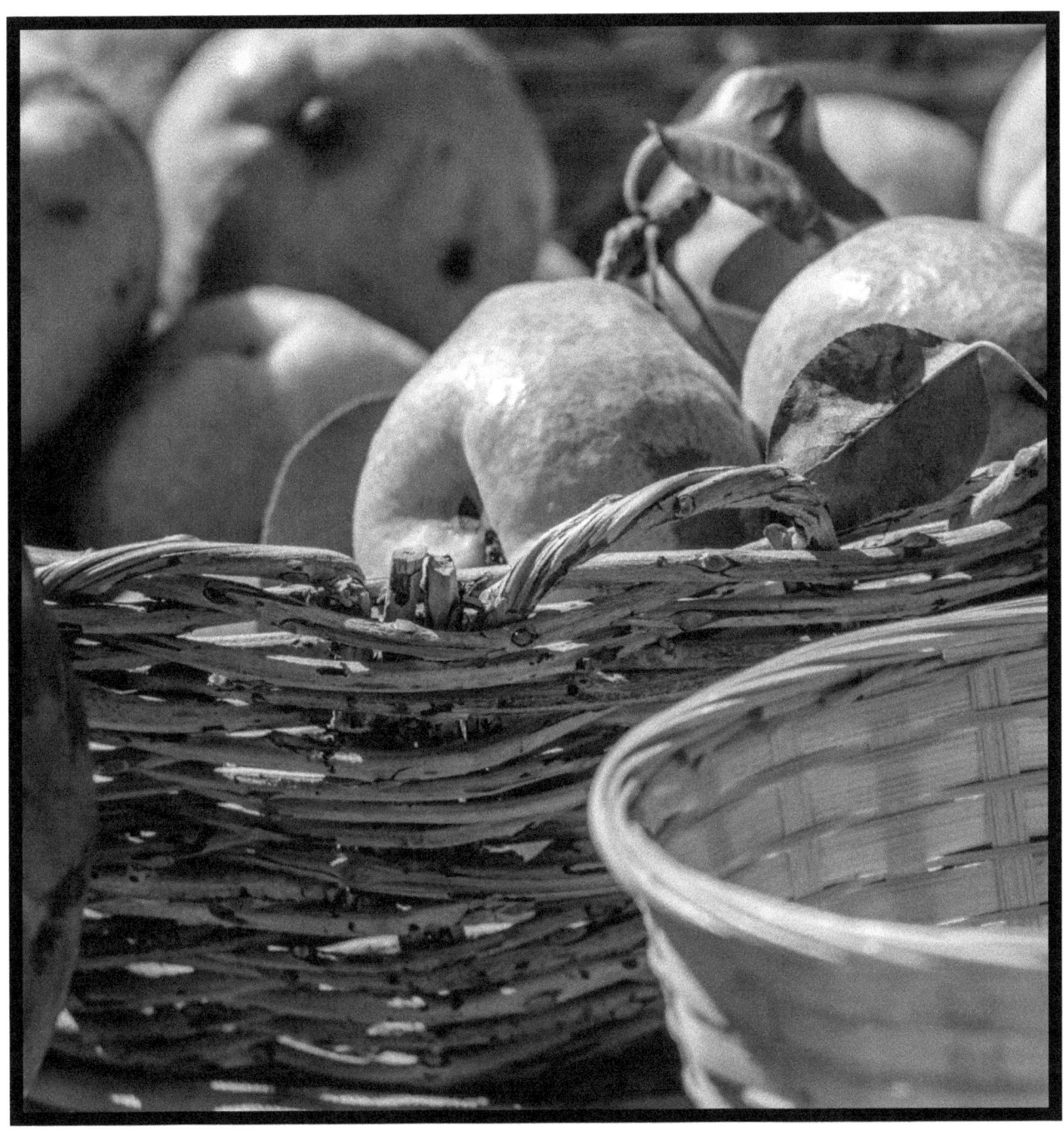

I used a minimal participation observational method during the collection of these photographs. My intentions were to uses a non-participant observational method, but I got roped into a conversation with a gentleman who told me about his plant based plastic containers. He said they were fully biodegradable; they were also 120% more expensive than normal plastic. He was adamant about doing good things for the environment, so he said they were worth it. He attempted to influence other farmers who used regular plastic containers to switch to the environmentally friendly alternative. This conversation was initiated because he caught me taking a picture of him.

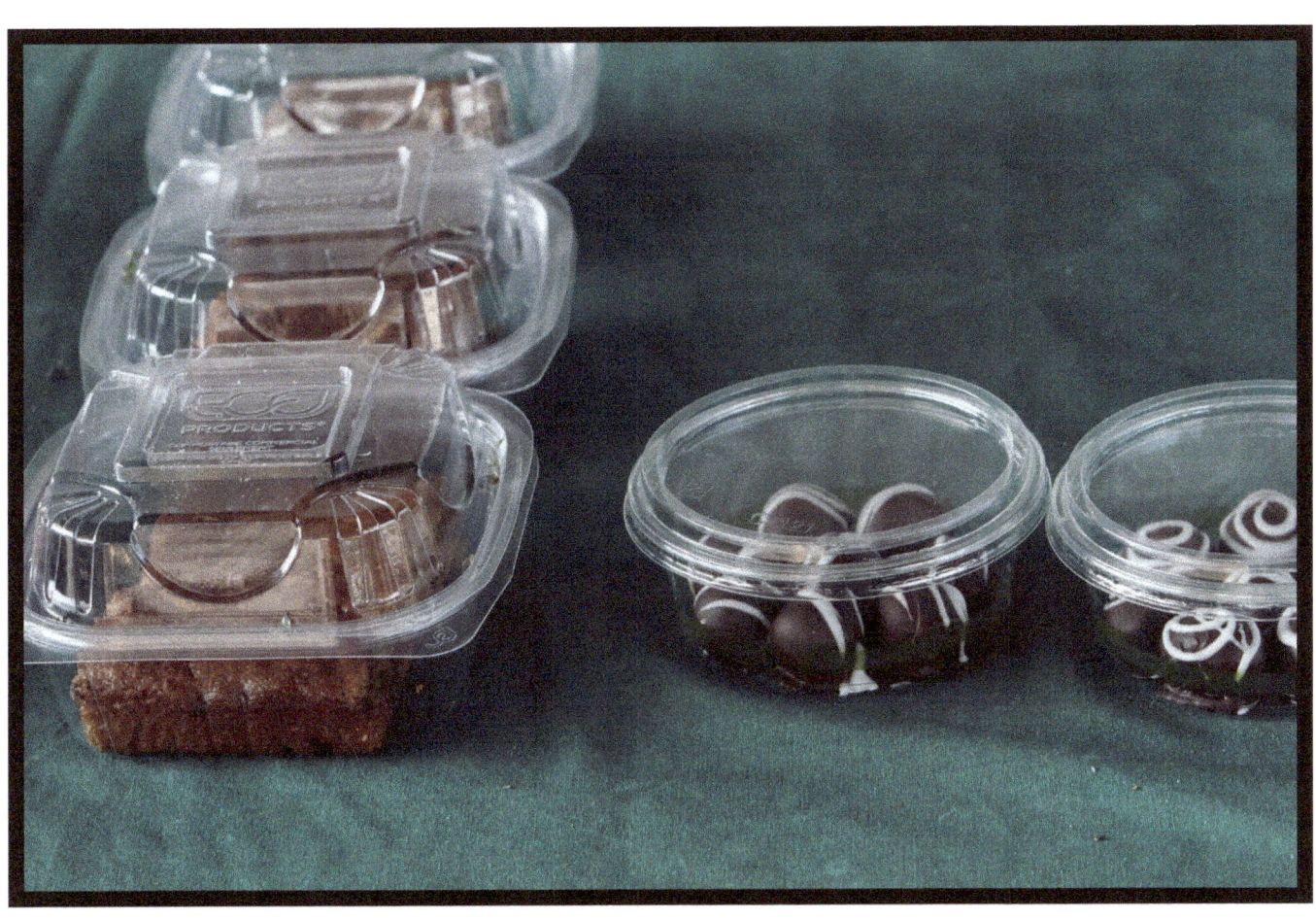

I had minor trouble visually, trying to convey the vessel as the primary subject in the photo. This was a minor hiccup I swiftly overcame. I felt no discomfort taking pictures of inanimate objects; unlike I did with taking pictures of people. I also had the most fleshed out idea of what I wanted to capture in my images.

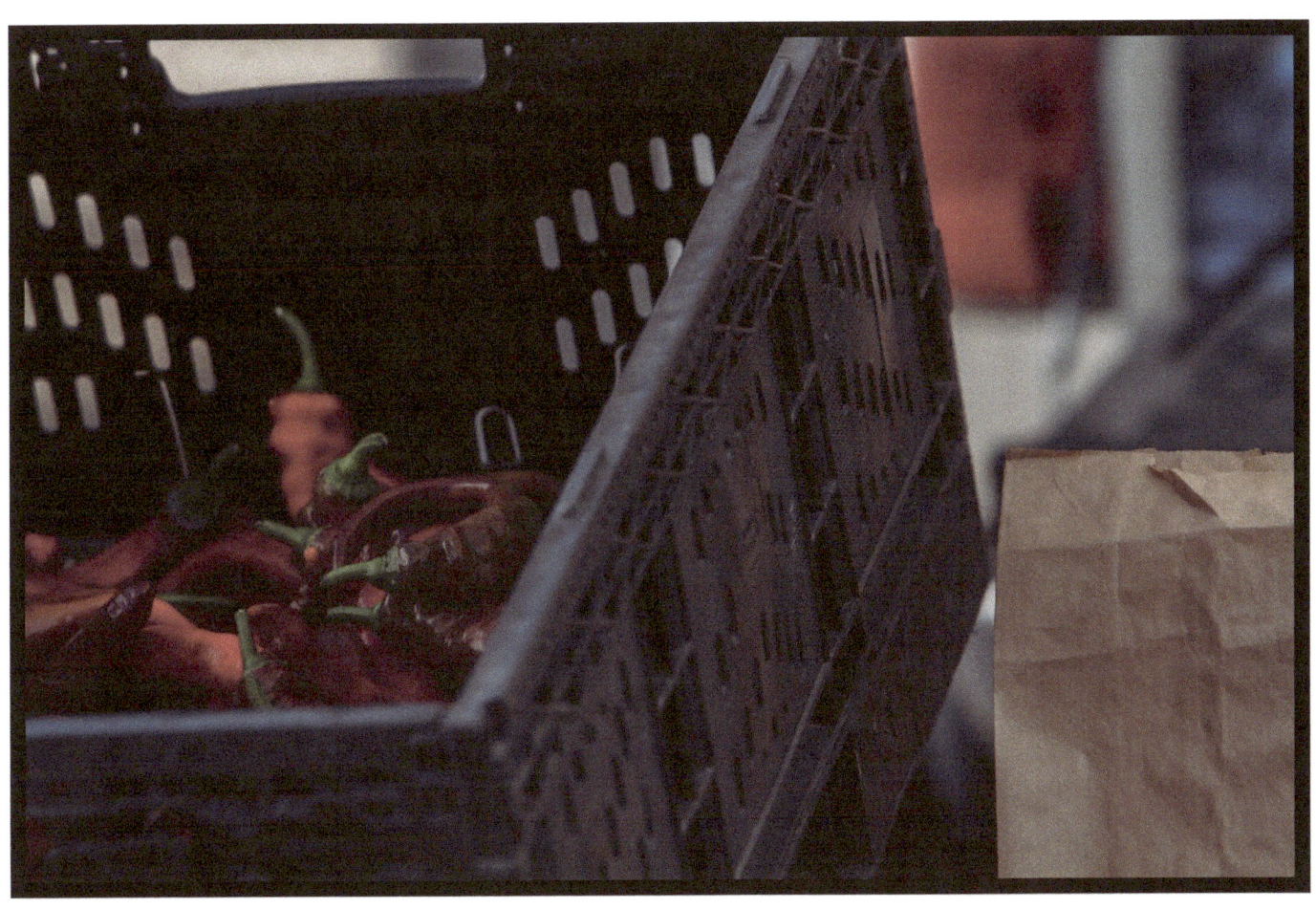

The majority of the vessels were either wicker baskets or thick plastic crates. Rarely did I see materials such as wood, metal, and occasionally cardboard to display whatever was being sold.

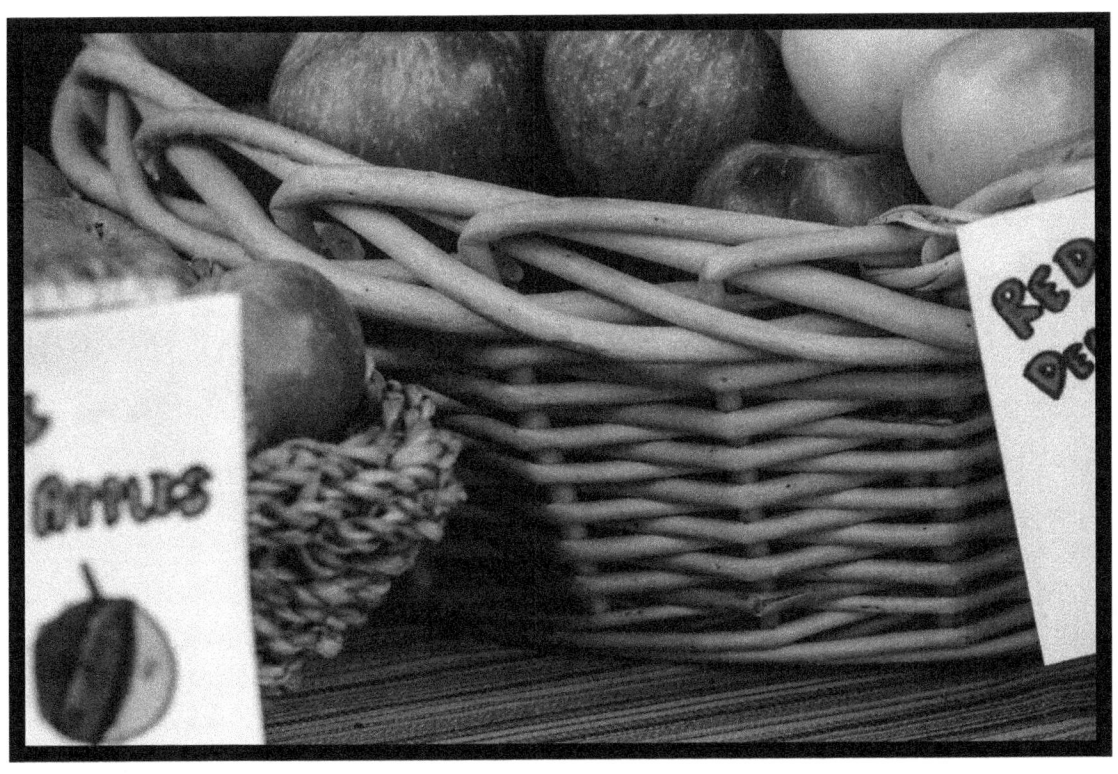

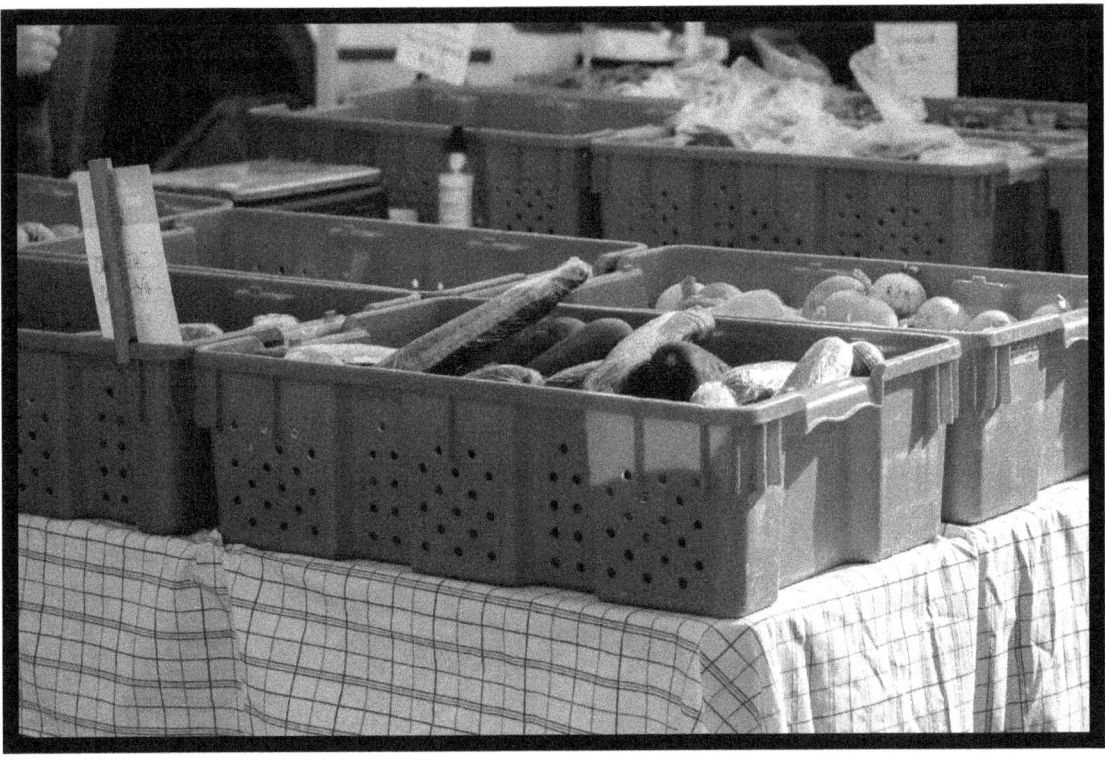

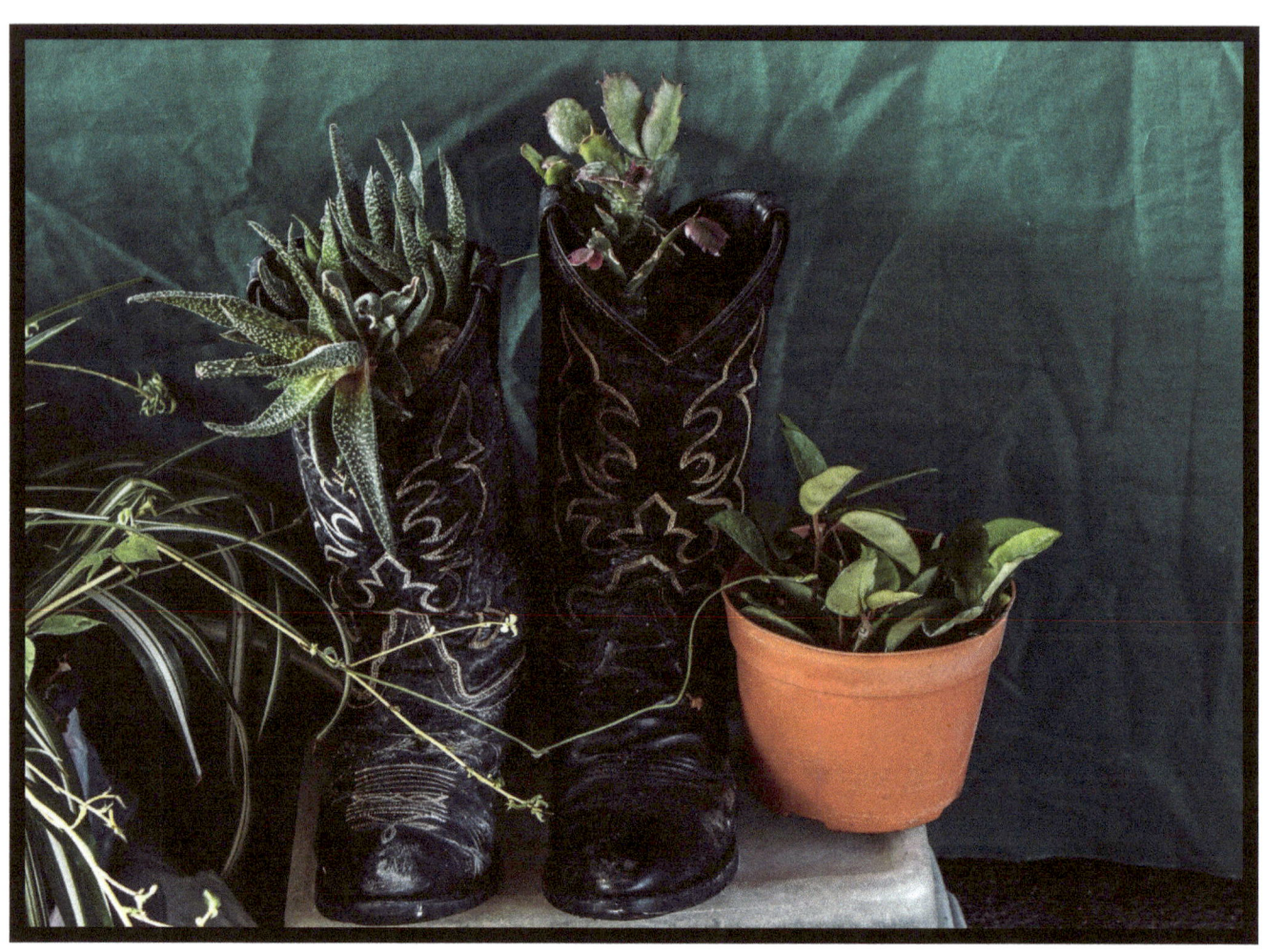

This [boot] was the most creative of vessels for displaying plants or anything for that matter. I didn't know if they were for sale; it was a unique and fun use of boots.

Comparing Raspberry Jam

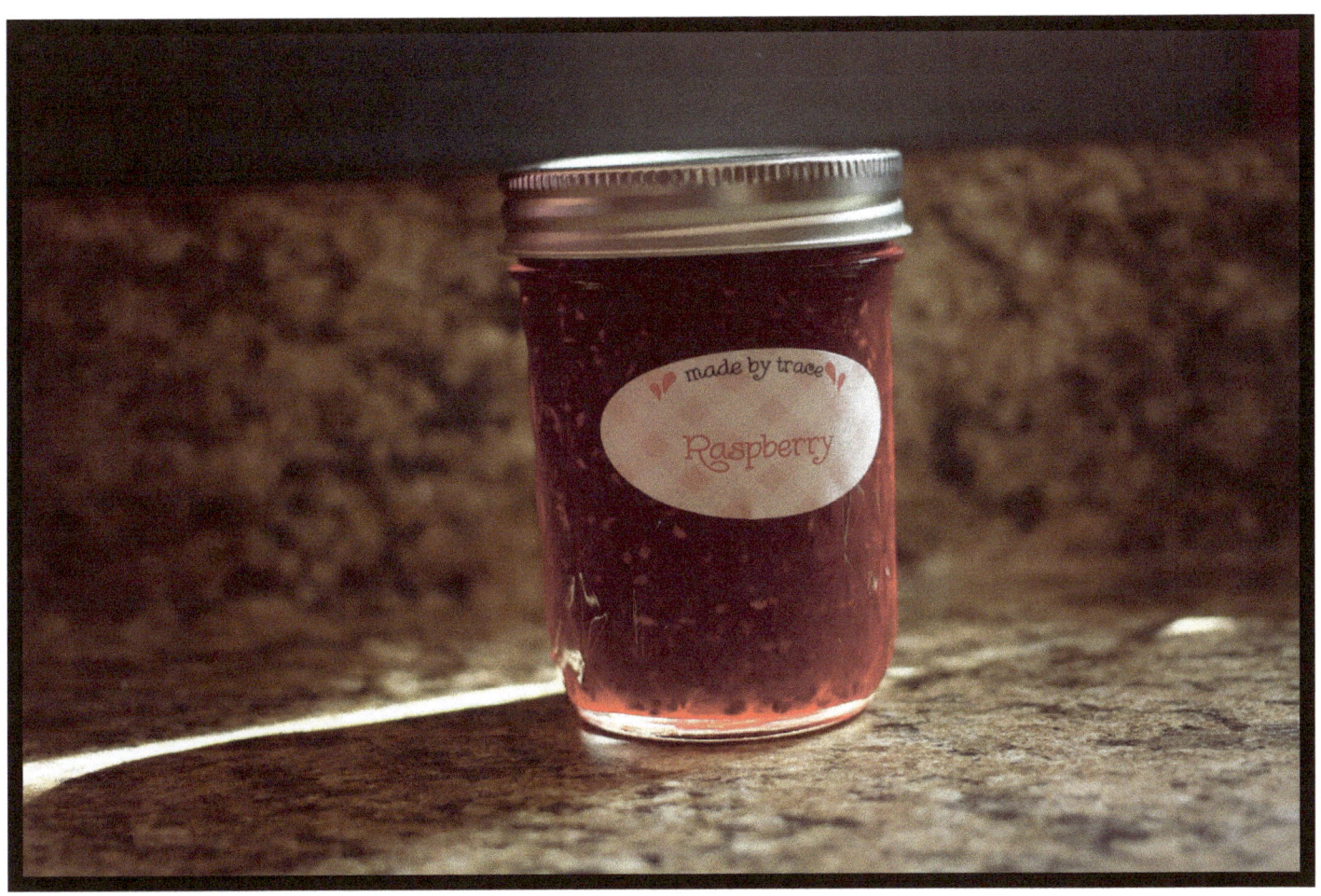

Every time I went to take photos at a farmers' market, I paid attention to what the farmers were selling; I did this to avoid taking pictures of people. Raspberry jam, sold by Mimbres Valley Farms (Silver City Farmers' Market), and raspberries sold by a kind gentleman at the Mimbres Valley Farmers' Market, both stood out among the foods. Raspberries have always been one of my favorite fruits, so that sparked my interest in studying both.

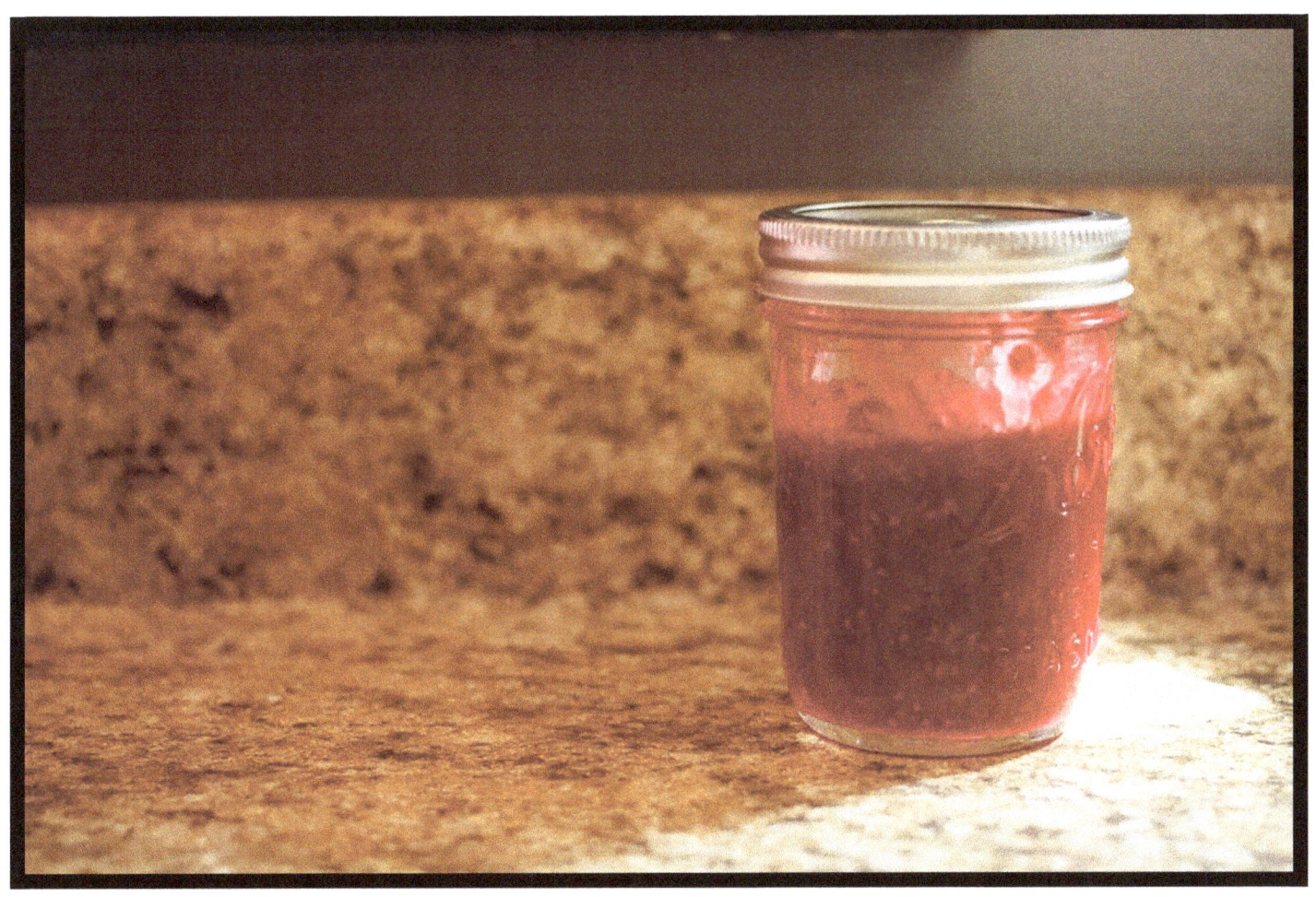

I was lucky to see the person normally selling raspberries, at the Mimbres valley farmers market; he was also selling jam. This allowed me to do a direct comparison of the jams.

I decided to approach the subject using biological research methods. I took seeds from both jams and looked at them under a microscope. I observed seed size, cell composition, color, and the overall look of the jam.

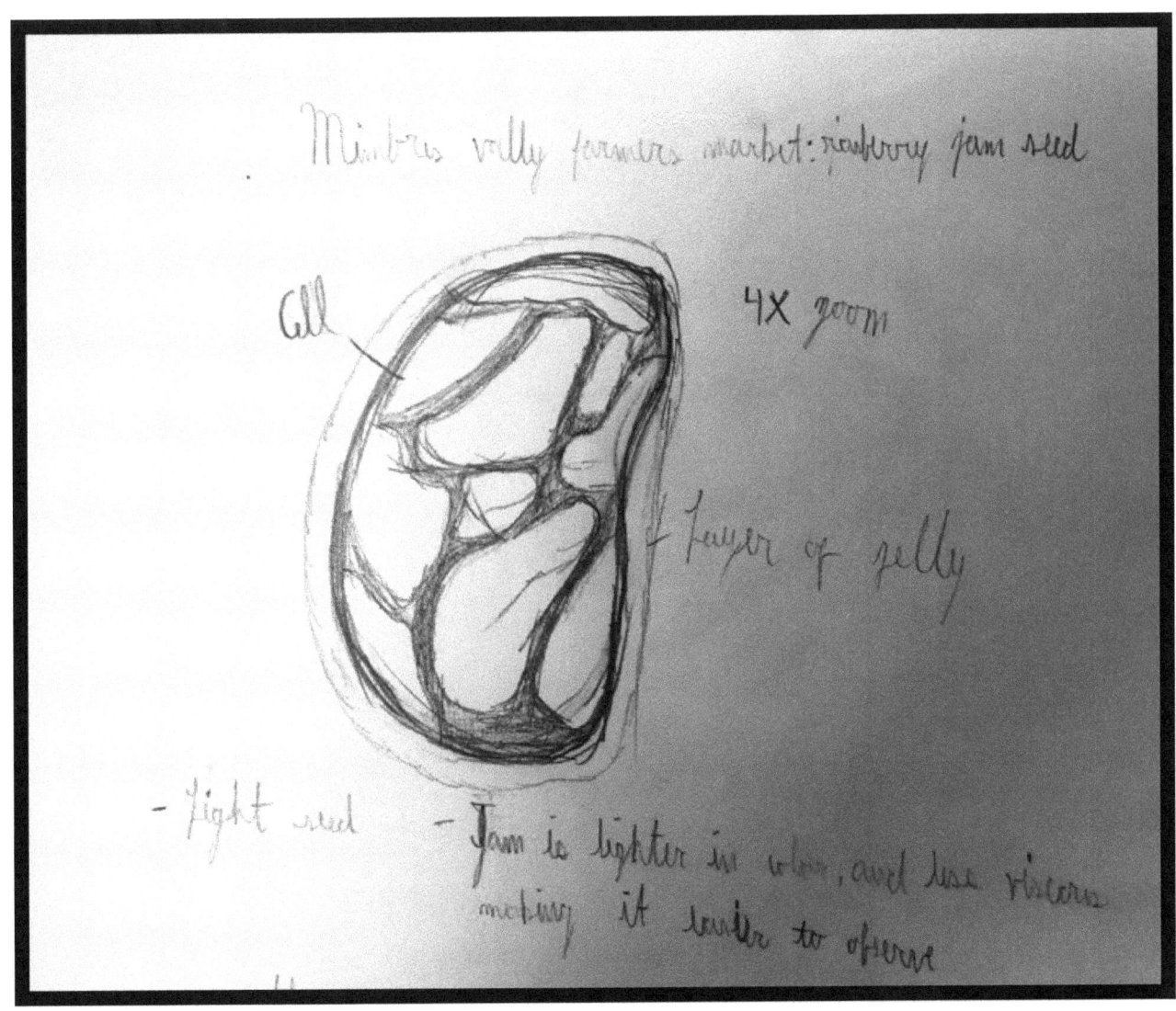

This is a rough sketch of a seed from the jam I bought from the Mimbres valley Farmers' Market. The seed was lighter in color, which made it easier to observe under a microscope. It was comprised of larger cells, and was the smallest of the seeds. In the jam itself, there was an abundance of what seemed like hairs scattered throughout the jelly. This was something I didn't see in the other jam.

Drawing conclusions based on the data I collected was difficult. The most I could hypothesize about was how big the raspberry was based on the seed, and how the jam may have been mixed based on viscosity and other material in the jam.

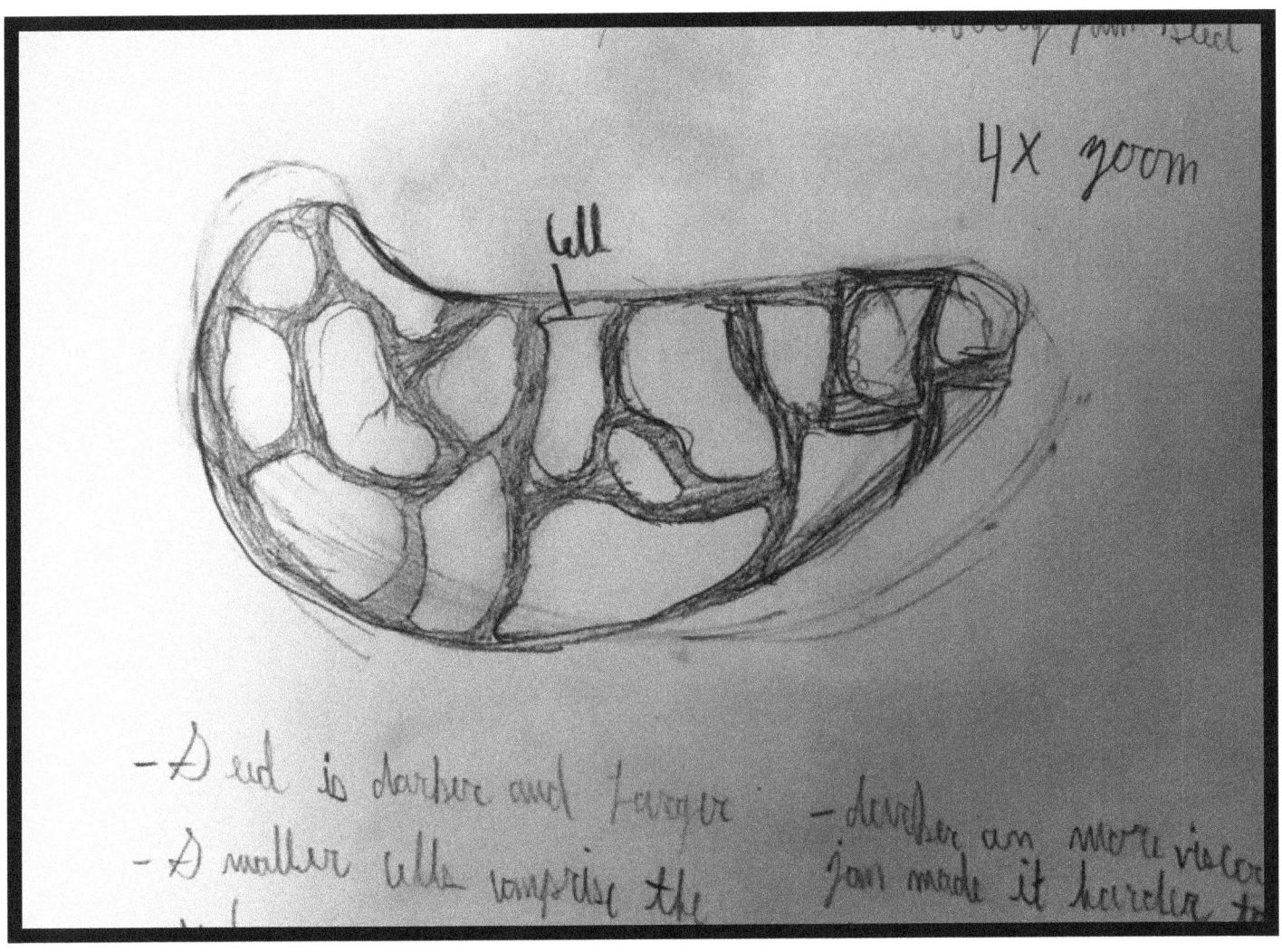

This is a sketch of a seed from the jam bought from the Silver City Farmers' Market. It was darker in color making observing under a microscope more difficult, since the cell walls weren't as easy to identify. It was the larger of the two, and the cells of the seed were smaller than the cells making up the smaller seed.

Comparing Cucumbers

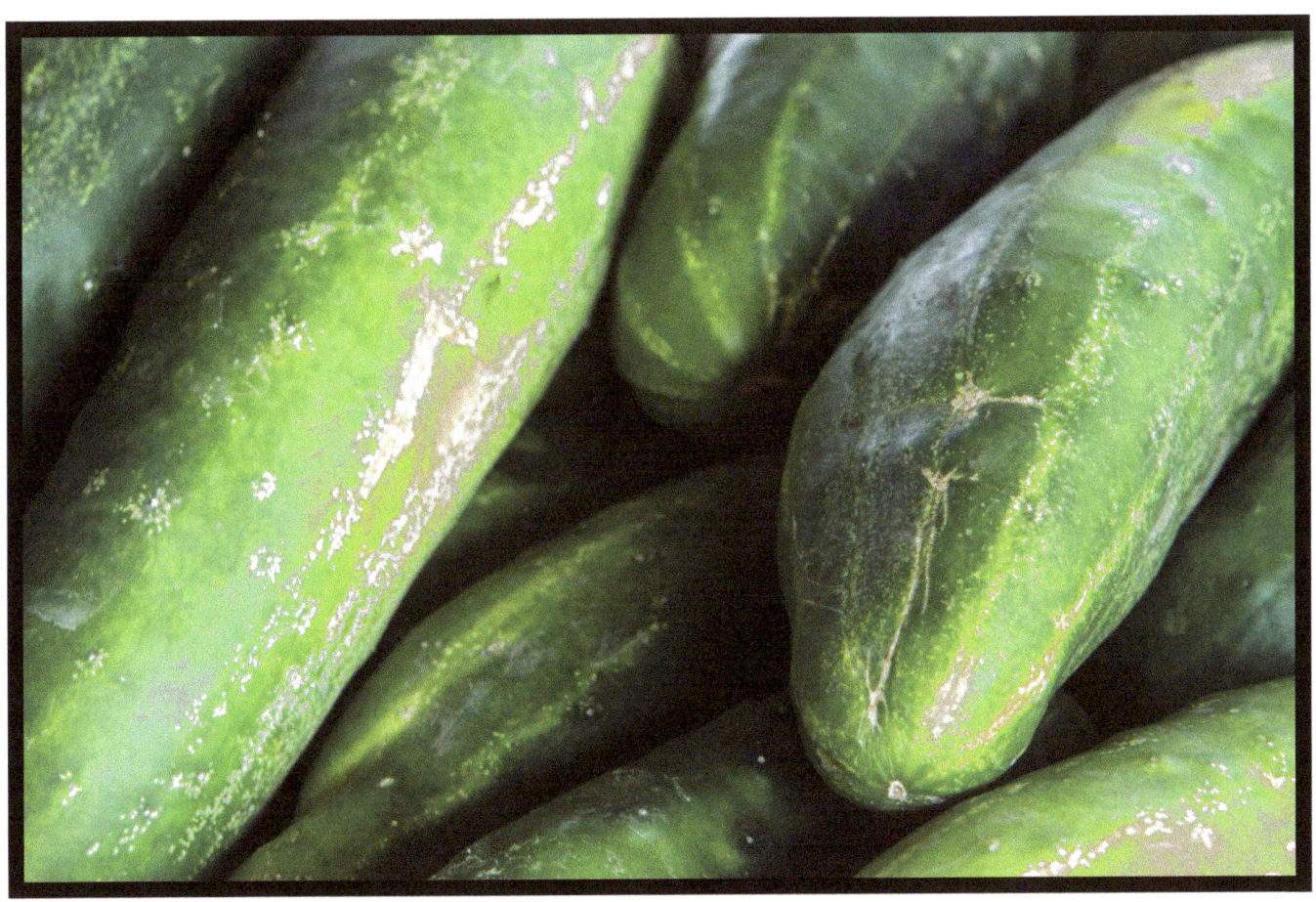

When I was looking for produce to compare, at the Silver City Farmers' Market, I noticed multiple growers selling cucumbers. Two of cucumbers were grown out in a field using well water; another cucumber was grown using hydroponics.

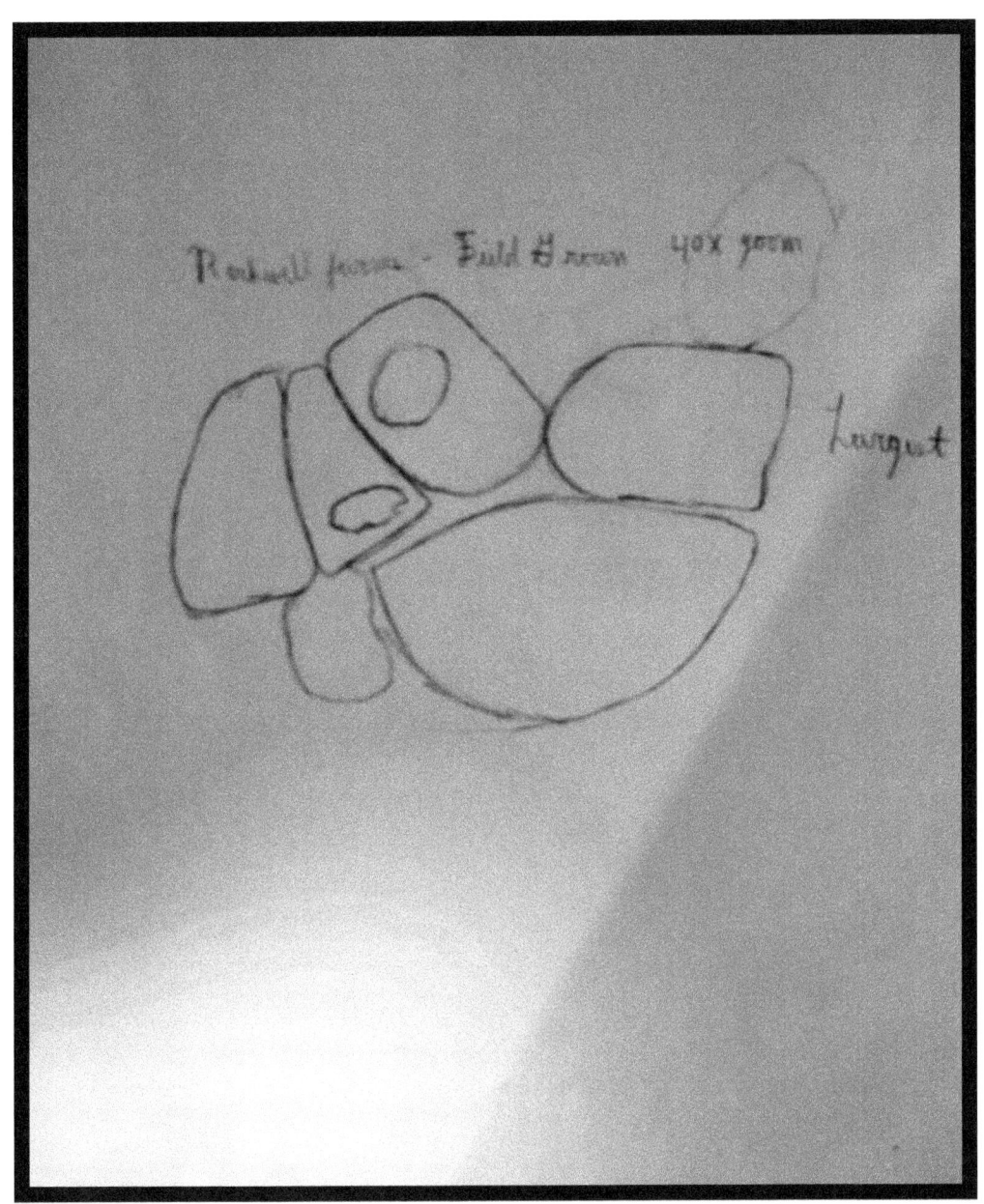

These are the skin cells of a cucumber bought from, Mimbres Valley Farms. It was grown in a field using well water, and was very short and stumpy which made it great for pickling, I was told. The cells comprising the skin were the largest of the 3, and the cells had little recognizable organization when compared to the others.

I approached the subject using biological methods I. I tore small pieces of skin off the cucumber using a pair of tweezers so I could better observe the skin under a microscope. I looked at cell size, organization, and moisture of the cucumber.

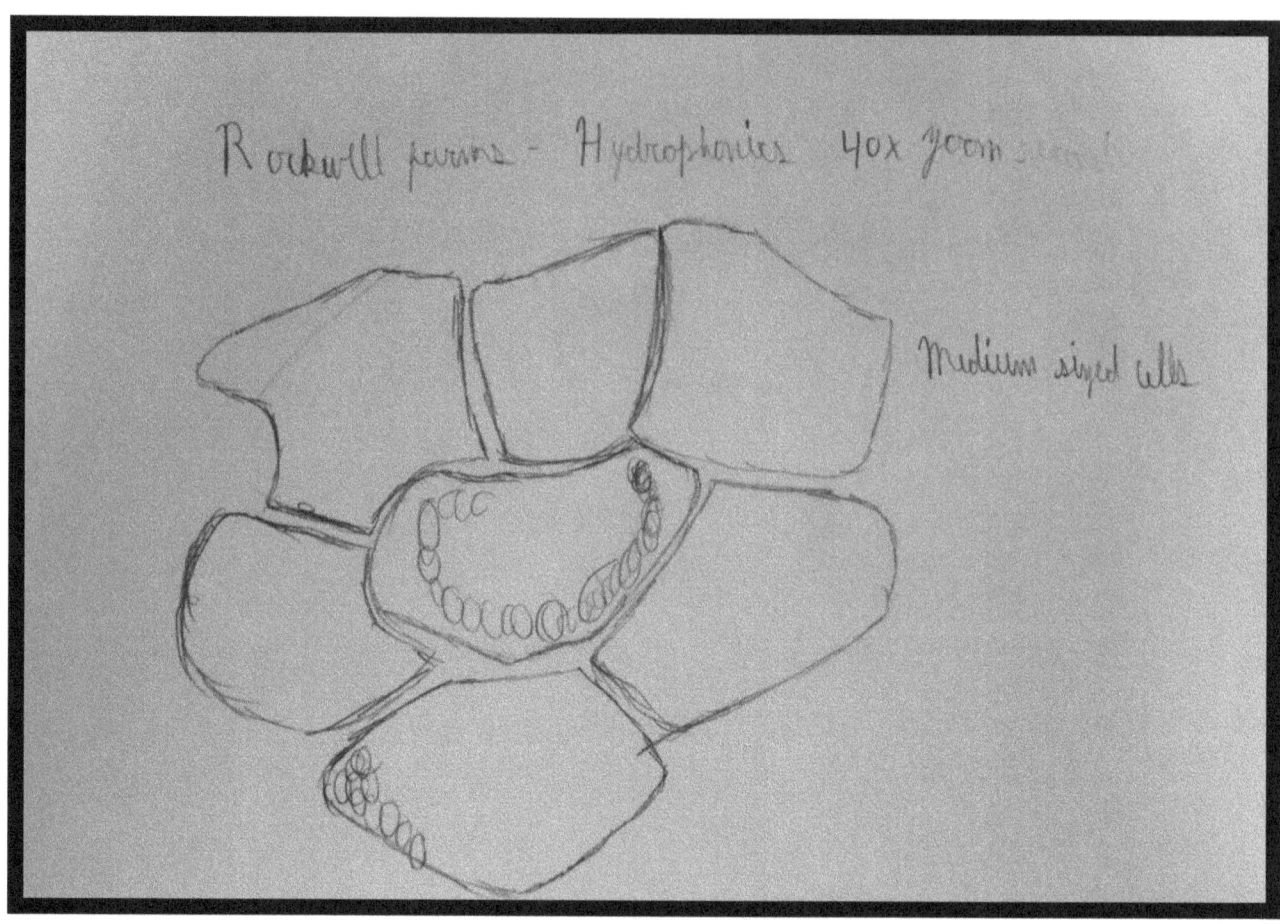

The skin cells of this cucumber came from Rockwell Farms (located in Deming, NM), and was grown using hydroponics. This cucumber was the skinniest, physically, out of the three, and also had the highest water content out of the bunch. The cells of the skin had a much higher level of recognizable organization compared to the Mimbres Valley Farm's cucumber. Additionally, the cells were about 50% smaller.

I had difficulty-generating hypothesis based on the information I gathered. One of the conclusions I jumped to was: *the cucumber with the highest level of water content was the one grown using hydroponics. I assumed this was due to the cucumber's 24-hour access to water. I also concluded that the field grown cucumbers had a similar shape, due to the way they were grown.*

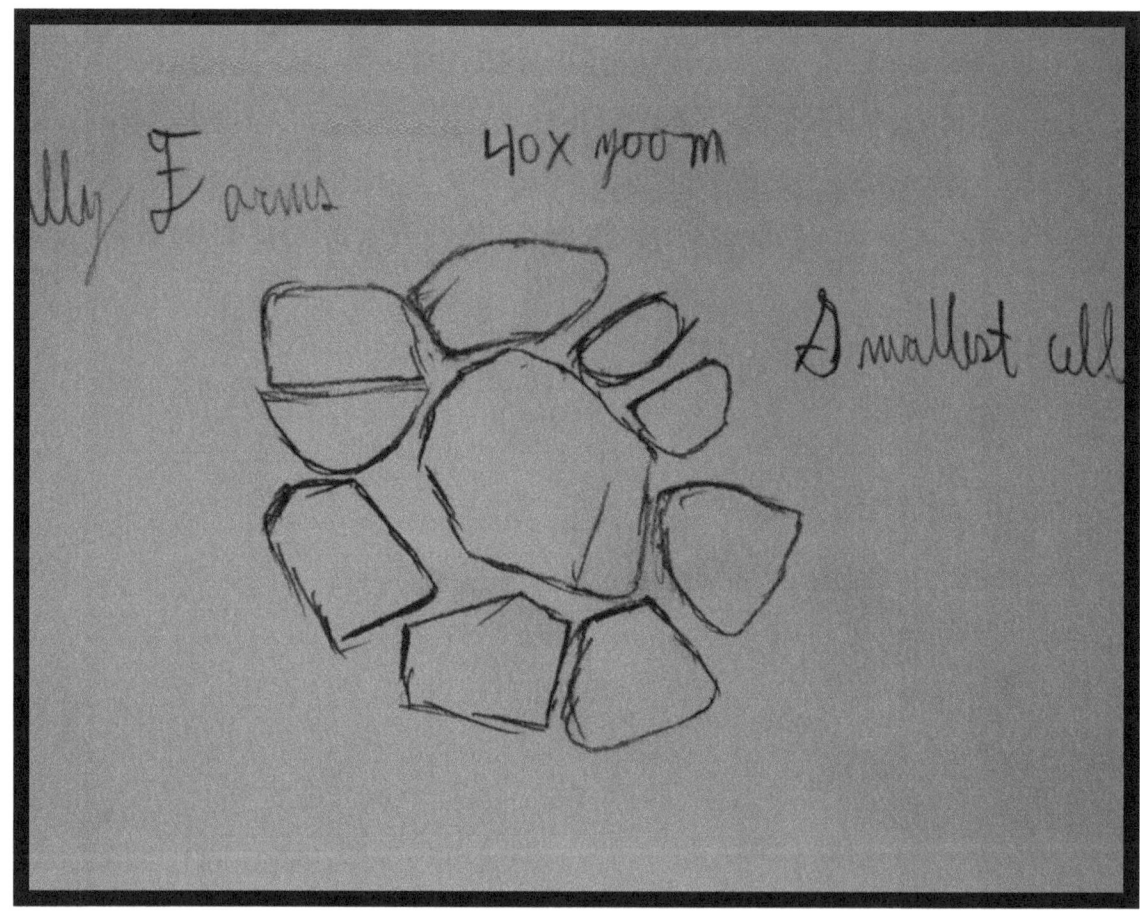

These are the skin cells from a field grown cucumber bought from, Rockwell Farms. The cells of this cucumber were the smallest out of the three, which I didn't expect. In regards to recognizing the organization, the cells were similar to the cucumber grown using hydroponics. The cucumber also looked similar to the one bought from Mimbres valley Farms, which is why I didn't expect the cellular organization and size to differ so heavily.

Generative Research

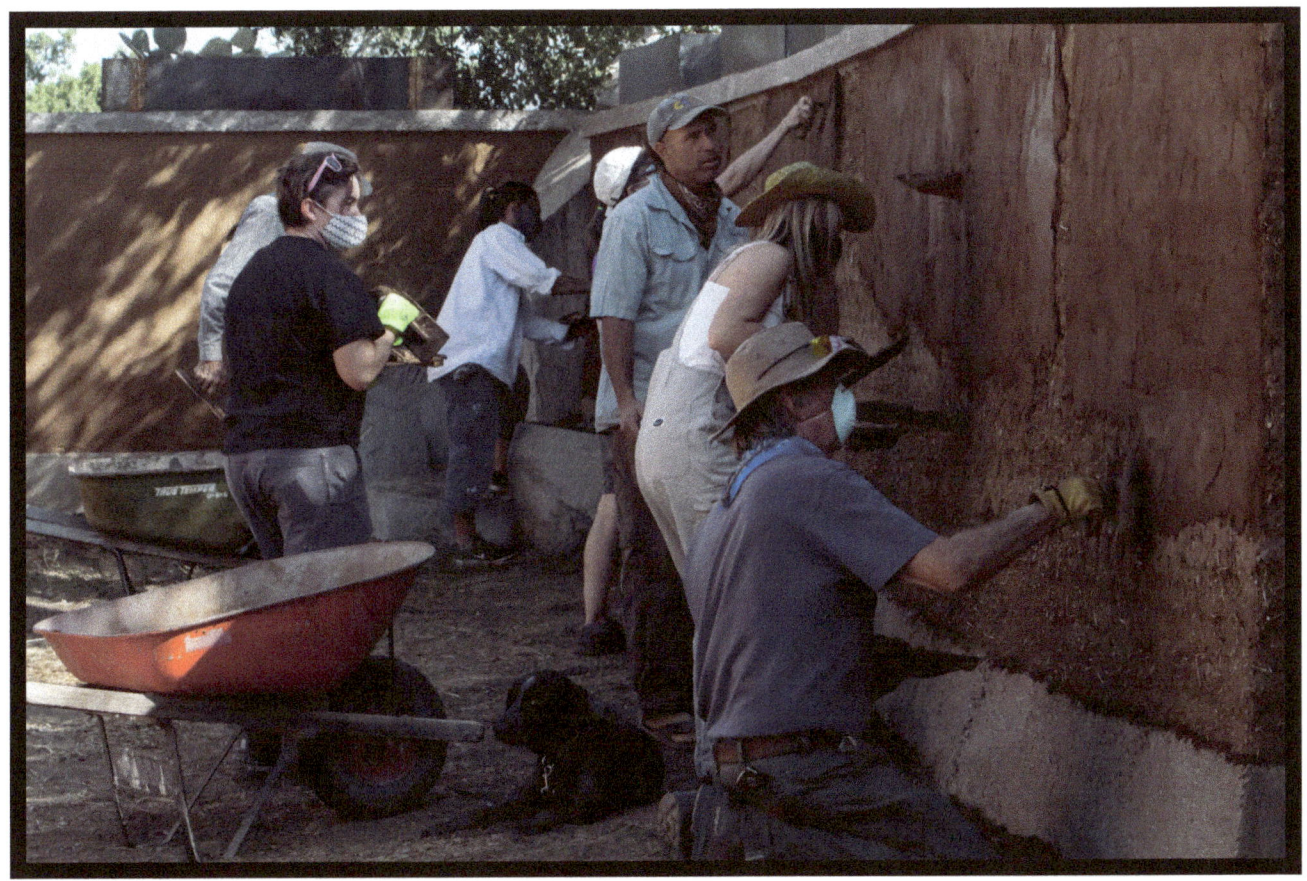

I caught sight, while driving to the Mimbres Valley Farmers' Market, a clay workshop that happened to be taking place. The workshop participants were mudding walls in the back of an old building. The main event I focused on, with my camera, were the participants' hands; the action of the hands was the only experience grabbing my attention.

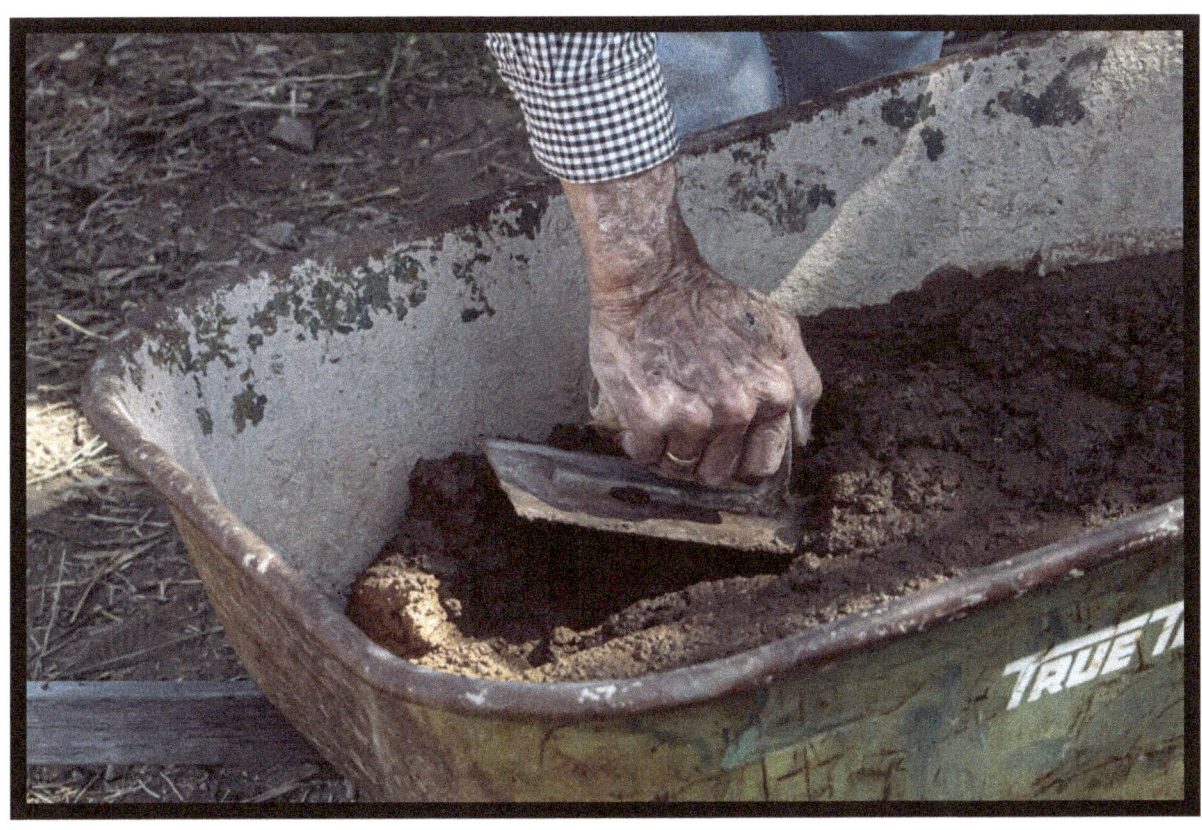

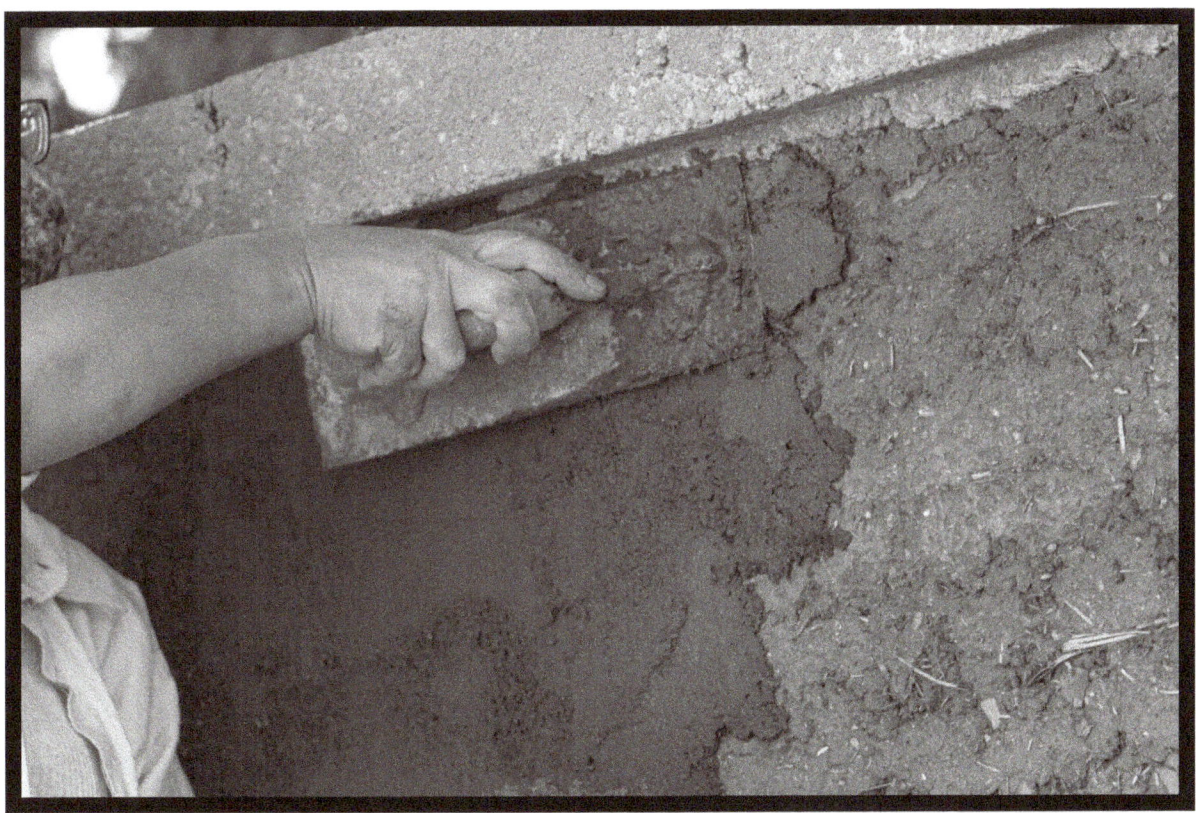

Seeing something being built for the community, with hands, made me wonder: *are there other ways hands are used to help build a community?*

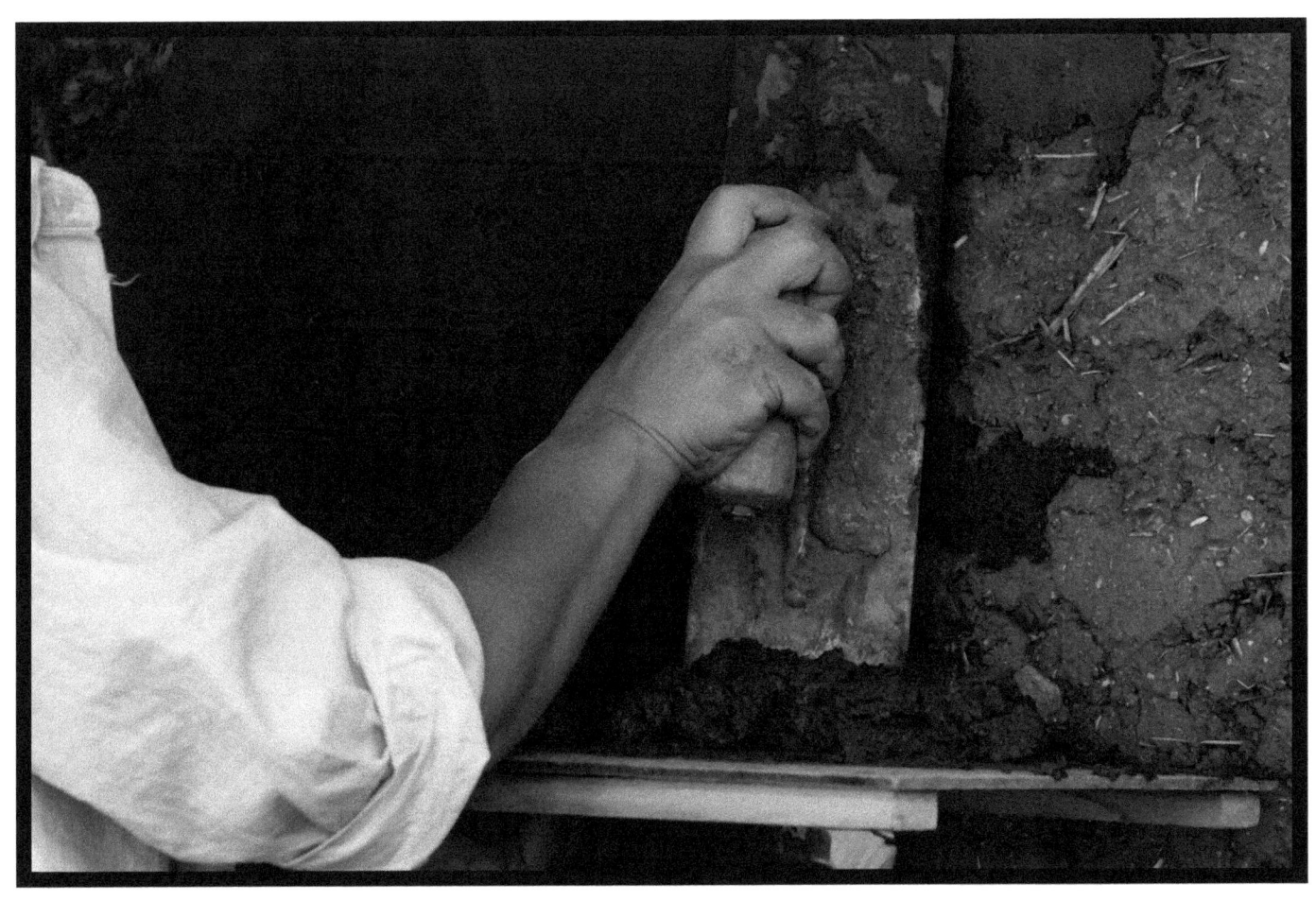

I remembered observing hands, minutely exploring the farmers' markets. At the time, I was just trying to avoid making eye contact with strangers. I had no intention for them to influence my future attention(s).

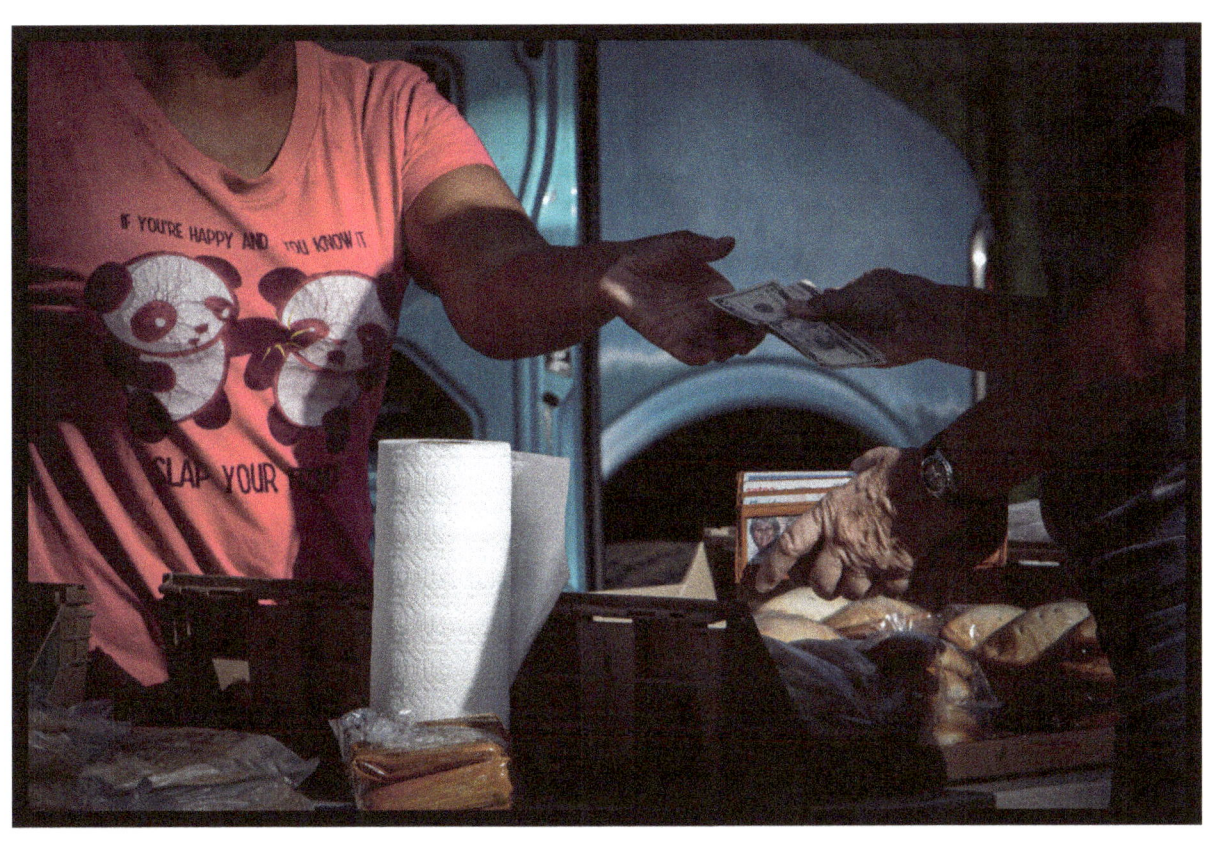

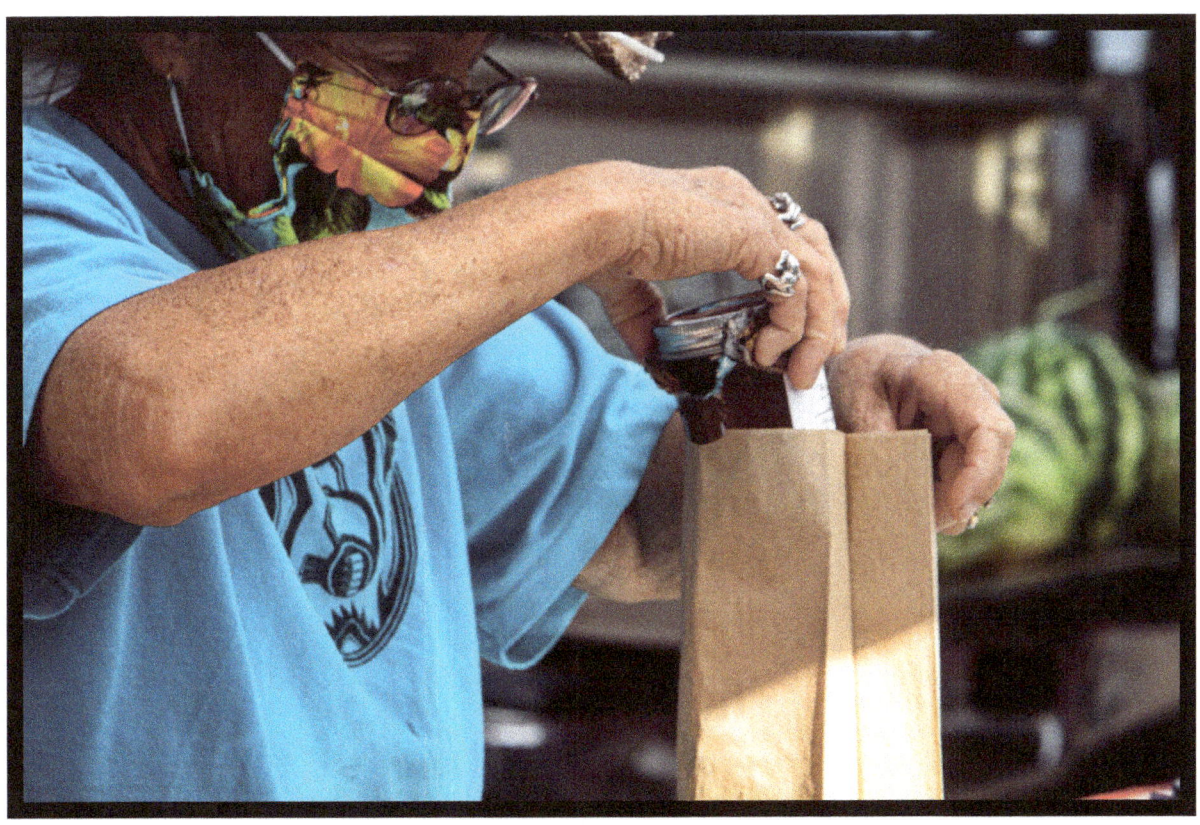

Thinking about the photos I took at the farmers market [in a new context] made me think about how much the human hand has a part in growing local businesses and economy. The flow of goods and money are essential to economic growth, and the human hand is one of the main facilitators.

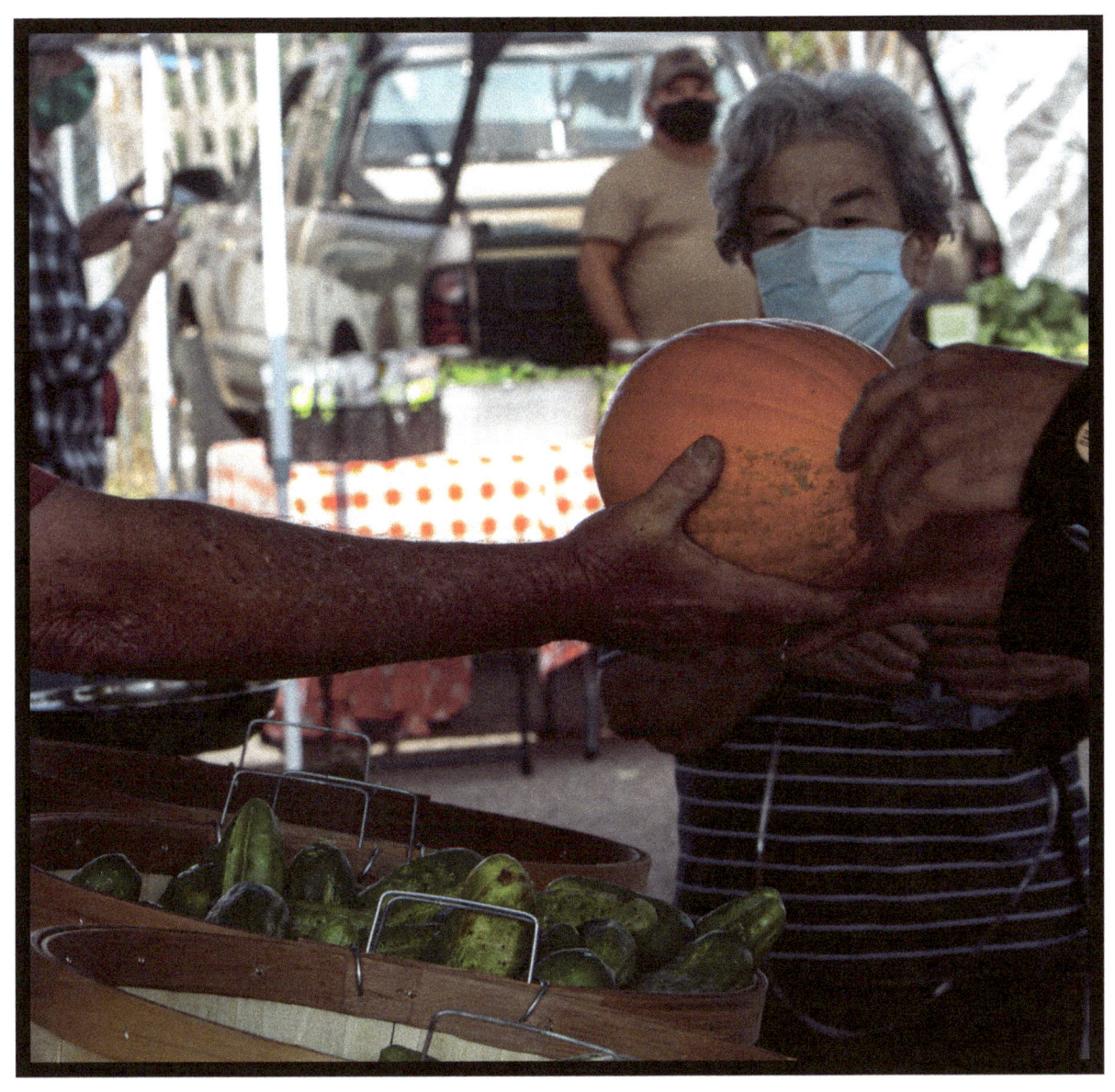

It really makes me think about how instrumental the human hand is in building a community. Hands extend to build houses, make exchanges happen at a farmers market, or even preparing food at a bakery.

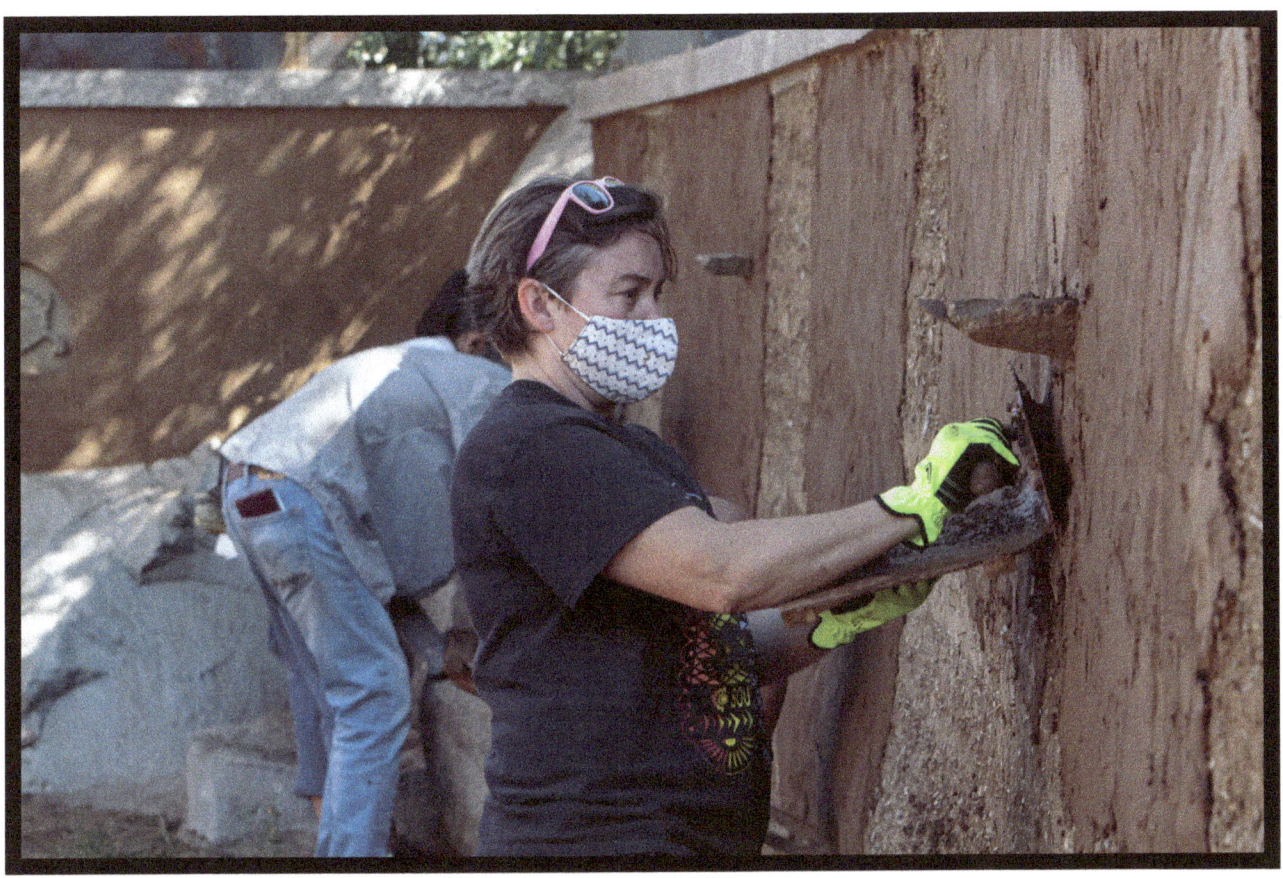

The bottom line - human hands play a part in almost everything we do and that should never be forgotten. Even nowadays, when so many people are stuck at home, we are still responsible for operating a keyboard.

For Future Reference

If I were to do it all over again, I would have tried to buck up the courage to interact verbally with people at the Farmers' Market. I'm curious as to what insights people may or may not have had about any of the patterns I noticed. After all, a farmers' market is a great place to socialize.

If I were to introduce someone to that type of fieldwork, I would tell them two things: I would tell them, "capture images that convey [clearly] what you are observing, and try not to be afraid to ask people questions".